Disciple Development Lifecycle Guidebook

DR. BRIAN GERARD FITE

Copyright ©2024 Dr. Brian Gerard Fite
All rights reserved.
ISBN: 979-8-9902474-0-6
No part of this document may be reproduced without written permission from
Blessed Coming & Going Productions
BCG158@Yahoo.com

Dedication

This work is dedicated to every believer in Yeshua who knew in their heart that salvation was not the end but the beginning of a powerful journey of growth and transformation to become everything Yeshua has for their new life in Him. May you become a Disciple who makes Disciples.

TABLE OF CONTENTS

Introduction to Spiritual Age as a Disciple Development Lifecycle ……………… 5

Unborn Again Development (Spiritual Age is 0) ……………………………………… 9
      Ministry Level ………………………………………………………………………………… 10

Born Again (New) Disciple Development (Spiritual Age is Day 1 – 2 years) …… 12
      Ministry Level   13
      Outline - Grace   15
      Outline - Prayer   24

Early Disciple Development (Spiritual Age is 2 – 5 years) - ……………………… 34
      Ministry Level   36
      Outline – Helps   37

Middle Disciple Development (Spiritual Age is 6 – 12 years) ………………… 50
      Ministry Level   52
      Outline - Giving   52

Adolescent Disciple Development (Spiritual Age is 13 – 20 years) …………… 89
      Ministry level   90
      Outline - Volunteering   91

Early Adulthood Disciple Development (Spiritual Age is 21 – 34 years) ……… 94
      Ministry Level   95
      Outline - Evangelism   96

Adult Disciple Development (Spiritual Age is 35 – 69 years) ………………… 170
      Ministry Level   171
      Outline – Spiritual Warfare   172

Senior Disciple Development (Spiritual Age is 70 – 80 years) ………………… 186
      Ministry Level   187
      Outline - Accountability   187

What is needed to be a community making disciples? ……………………… 193

INTRODUCTION TO SPIRITUAL AGE AS A DISCIPLE DEVELOPMENT LIFE CYCLE

First, let's understand two important definitions:

A DISCIPLE… is someone who has consciously committed to receive the free grace of God through Yeshua and has determined to learn, live, and share the teachings of Yeshua as their standard to live by.

DISCIPLE MAKING… is the process of informing unbelievers of the grace of Yahweh. If they confess Yeshua as their Lord and Savior, then there is an investment to develop them into mature disciples. A Mature disciple's investment in new and young disciples is called Disciple Making: the act or process of making and maturing disciples.

This Disciple Development Lifecycle is a roadmap for the development of disciples. The commission of Yeshua is to make disciples of all nations.

This document outlines the stages of disciple development using a concept called *Spiritual Age.*

> *Spiritual Age is intended to measure the spiritual growth and development of Christian disciples. It is a subjective measurement because it is not possible to know all of the factors that impact spiritual development and lifestyle.*

The measurement will be more effective based on the information available about past experiences and current levels of consistency and commitment to the Kingdom of God.

The disciples in scripture developed at a faster pace than has been documented in this process. This could be attributed to the fact that they resigned from all other activities and responsibilities to solely focus on being and making disciples, which most Christian disciples are not in a position to do. Disciples must learn how to balance school, work, family, and social involvements while developing as disciples of Yeshua. This means that development will occur at a slower pace than the disciples in scripture, and development will look different than for other disciples in the community.

Everyone should begin their Disciple Development Lifecycle at the point of accepting Yeshua as their personal Savior and Lord. However, this is an idea but does not address the reality that many of us have been committed to Yeshua as Savior and Lord without a roadmap like this. Therefore, it is important for disciples to know and understand the stages of development that they must experience and what disciples can expect from the community of disciples.

The assessment of *Spiritual Age* must be completed by your spiritual leader. The assumption is that your spiritual leader is directly connected to the vision that you have been positioned to assist and has observed your development and commitment to God's Kingdom. Your spiritual leader should know the role you can have in the advancement of God's vision so that their determination of your **Spiritual Age** will assist in designing a development plan for you to grow in your disciple-making community and the Kingdom of God. These stages are generalized. The spiritual leader is not bound by any of this information and must trust their wisdom and *Calling* to ultimately determine a **Spiritual Age.**

Using human development stages as a basis, the following Spiritual Development Stages have been established to provide context for Spiritual Ages. It is key that you understand serving in the Disciple Making Community must be a result of spiritual growth and development. Disciples must mature to serve in certain ministry roles. Growth and maturity must be the factors that determine your level of service to and for God.

UNBORN AGAIN DEVELOPMENT
(Spiritual Age is 0)

"Receiving Ministry...not yielded to Receive Salvation"

This is the stage of life before yielding to the grace of God through salvation. Just as with a fetus, this stage is important to how a disciple will grow and develop later in their spiritual life. It is important to understand the impact of prenatal care and events.

Events and decisions in this stage have a great impact on the rate of growth a disciple will have.

Many disciples struggle to understand the actions of the Disciple Making Community (church) during their *Unborn Again* stage. It is important to know that salvation is a clean start. God does not intend for disciples to hold to the events in life prior to accepting the grace of God, especially those that are negative and ungodly.

MINISTRY LEVEL

There is no service in this stage. They need to be exposed to the teachings of Yeshua and the love of the community. Their involvement with the community must be closely monitored to ensure that they understand that confession and commitment are necessary to become a member of the community. This must be clearly understood. These are Seekers who are not yet disciples.

They have not made a confession to Salvation, nor a commitment to Disciple Development or making.

Attendance and participation without confession and commitment are meaningless. The spiritual leader and community must understand that their focus and objective is to make disciples, not increase attendance and participation.

NOTES

BORN AGAIN (NEW) DISCIPLE DEVELOPMENT

(Spiritual Age – Day 1-2 Years)

"The building blocks are made...possibly the most important stage of development."

This is the stage when you have yielded to the grace of salvation. This stage of development is possibly the most important. This is the stage where the building blocks for growth are laid. It is important for the new disciple to invest in reading scripture and praying continually. One of the mistakes made at this stage is rushing the new disciple into the next stages before a strong foundation is developed.

The struggles of the *Unborn Again* Life must be addressed and defeated during infancy. Disciples struggle with behavior and events of their *Unborn Again* Life because they were not given time to form a meaningful foundation and receive release from the impacts of their *Unborn Again* Life.

> *New Disciples should be very limited in the role they are given. This stage is directly related to the time invested in salvation.*

Infancy development should take 18 months to 2 years. New Disciples need structure and discipline to form the necessary foundation for further spiritual growth. Many disciples did not develop appropriately in this stage; therefore, they struggled with consistency and commitment while believing they were growing spiritually. The spiritual leader should not give any consideration to ability or performance. It is important to allow this stage to take 18 months to 2 years so that the New Disciple learns to pray and read scripture regularly and continuously.

MINISTRY LEVEL

New Disciples are students. In this development stage, New Disciples are taught what grace is and how it has destroyed their past and opened possibilities for their future. New Disciples are given opportunities to testify about their transformation by grace. Additionally, they are assigned a mentor or placed in a group with other New Disciples so they can begin to demonstrate a willingness to share the Gospel and pray openly for their spiritual community. After the New Disciples learn grace, they will lay a stong foundation in prayer.

Understanding and consistency are formed.
Their focus is to learn the elements of prayer
and the meaning of Grace.

Correction is key for New Disciples because they are learning how to be committed disciples of Yeshua. Correction of New Disciples must be executed with love and patience.

Remember, their foundation is being laid; therefore, they must learn to embrace correction but not be defeated in the process.

As these disciples near the end of infancy, they can start to participate in ministries that have a very controlled environment, such as media, custodial tasks, lawn care, and maintenance. New Disciples must be supervised at all times so that mistakes and deficiencies can be addressed and corrected. The mentors and supervisors must have patience and be consistent, mature examples that the New Disciples can imitate.

In this stage use the bold topics to teach the new disciples about grace and prayer. This is not just for information. It is for implementation. As they learn what the scriptures teach they are to implement the teachings into their daily life.

Outline
GRACE

What is Grace?

The first understanding for all disciples is grace. The objective of this topic is to provide a basic understanding of what grace is and what it requires of us as disciples.

We present two definitions for grace:

- The unmerited favor, mercy, compassion, acceptance, kindness, graciousness, goodwill, and divine assistance of God.
- The divine life, power, and ability of God flowing and operating through us to give us the supernatural power and ability for ministry and sanctification.

GRACE TO RESTORE:

Grace is accessed in two ways: through salvation and repentance. Grace is to be understood as the loving response of our Father to the nature and activity of sin (John 3:16-21).

Disciples must focus on verses 17-21 to understand the impact of rejecting grace. Disciples are not perfect and will sin by thought, word, and action; therefore, disciples must understand repentance and the necessity of open and honest acknowledgment of our sins (James 5:13-16). We must practice confession regularly to defeat shame and distrust in the community of disciples. The Hebrew term for repentance is Teshuvah, which means *return,* as if turning back to something or someone you have strayed from. Repentance is not an apology; it is a request to be transformed while being allowed to return to Yahweh through grace provided by Yeshua. Confession is Part of our Testimony Process:

- Salvation – **John 3:16-21**
- Repentance – ***James 5:13-16*** (Confession tied to effective prayer)

> *"For God so loved the world that he gave his only Son, so that everyone who believes in him may not perish, but may have eternal life."* John 3:16 NRSV

> *"Therefore, confess your sins to one another and pray for one another, so that you may be healed. The prayer of the righteous is powerful and effective."* James 5:16 NRSV

GRACE TO FORGIVE:

Once God restores you, the expectation is that you will restore others through forgiveness – *Luke 6:32-49.*

Disciples are to forgive others so that the same measure of forgiveness will be given to them. Forgiveness is reciprocal.

Forgiveness is a choice. It is based on acknowledgment of wrongdoing. A person cannot be forgiven for a sin that they did not commit.

GRACE TO RELEASE:

The thoughts, feelings, hurts, and memories must be released – *John 8:31-38.*

The impact and memory of sin must be temporary.

Disciples are not to invest in lingering guilt. Disciples are to be grieved to the point of repentance, but forgiveness is the standard for Disciples. To live redeemed and offer redemption to others through Yeshua the Christ.

FREE & FORWARD:

On the day you receive the grace of God, you are free and must immediately move forward – *Romans 8:1-8*. The life and journey of a disciple are always focused on 'forward.'

> *Disciples must invest in forward thinking and behavior. The power of grace is to forgive and release.*

This allows disciples to focus on moving forward for the Kingdom of God. Disciples are to be actively involved in sharing grace with all humankind because everyone needs an opportunity to receive and live under the grace of God. Either through salvation or repentance, there is no condemnation for those who are in Yeshua the Christ.

GRACE MAKES YOU A NEW CREATION:

Disciples must embrace being a new creation. This means we are new from when we were created. Disciples are not made new from the point of salvation. Grace covers our entire life. <u>**2 Corinthians 5:16 - 6:10.**</u>

This is how shame and guilt are defeated: Understanding that grace covers everything we have done against God.

GRACE MUST BE SHARED:

Everything grace does for you must be given to everyone who has wronged you. Disciples must understand the importance of giving grace to those who wrong us. It is not enough to seek forgiveness when we are wronged. Equally important is offering grace to those who acknowledge they have wronged us. This was so important that Yeshua included it in his model for prayer. **Luke 11:4**

> *"And forgive us our debts, as we also have forgiven our debtors. And do not bring us to the time of trial, but rescue us from the evil one." Luke 11:4 NRSV*

GRACE TO SHARE THE TRUTH:

As free followers of Yeshua we are empowered by the truth. We cannot and will not lie for any reason.

> *We are truth tellers. Grace forgives; therefore, lying is a rejection of Grace.*

Our Father is willing to forgive if we acknowledge and confess; therefore, why should disciples lie? Disciples must live by truth daily and especially in the community of disciples. Lies cannot be tolerated because there is no reason for a disciple to lie. Grace is available to everyone. Baptism and Communion should not be rituals; they are an opportunity to express the true impact of grace on a disciple.

> *"And you will know the truth, and the truth will make you free."*
> John 8:32 NRSV

- Truth is different from opinion
- Truth is to release, not hurt. Learn to be direct and compassionate at the same time. **John 8:32**
- Testimony is to tell the truth about yourself regularly (the best way to confess).
- Baptism is the first public testimony of our surrender to the Lordship of Yeshua.
- Communion is our regular testimony of the reality of Yeshua.

As disciples of Yeshua the Christ, we must invest in our witness through multiple methods of testimony.

GRACE TO BE EMPOWERED – <u>1 John 4:1-6.</u>

Forward movement must be accompanied by empowerment. Disciples must always seek to be greater, more productive, and more effective for the Kingdom. There are false teachers who will seek to use bondage, guilt, greed, and ambition to alter the sincere meaning and power of grace.

> *Our new life in Yeshua the Christ is designed to be a growth process of empowerment.*

GRACE IS A LIFESTYLE THAT PRODUCES OBEDIENCE AND IMPACT - <u>Matthew 13:1-23.</u>

> *Disciples live in obedience to Yeshua by striving to multiply disciples every day.*

This is our standard and lifestyle to reproduce Disciples.

Outline

Prayer

Power of Prayer

LEARN THE FLOW YESHUA TAUGHT – THE LORD'S PRAYER:

This was not to be recited. Yeshua gave the disciples this foundation for understanding how to pray and what the focus of our prayers should be.

- **Matthew 6:7-15**
- **Luke 11:1-13**

It is to be used as a model to structure the flow of your prayers.

PRAYER IS A PRIVILEGE – _Ephesians 3:14-21_

To be able to go to our Father for direction, correction, comfort, and peace is one of the privileges of being a disciple. We must respect and appreciate this privilege by utilizing it regularly and continuously.

> *"And that Christ may dwell in your hearts through faith, as you are being rooted and grounded in love. I pray that you may have the power to comprehend, with all the saints, what is the breadth and length and height and depth." Ephesians 3: 17 – 18 NRSV*

PRAYER IS A REQUIREMENT – _Luke 18:1-17._

This scripture contains two parables and a teaching. In the first parable, the need to always pray and not lose heart (verse 1) is also evident in verses 7-8: to pray continually for justice. The second parable is about two men praying; verse 13 tells us to have humility when we pray and not to think that we are better than others because we pray. The final teaching confirms the importance of humility and innocence in verse 17. He is not saying people must accept salvation as a child or youth. He is saying disciples must have humility and innocence like a child.

> *"Will not God grant justice to his chosen ones who cry to him day and night?*
> *Will he delay long in helping them?"*
> *Luke 18:7 NRSV*

PRAYER IS A TWO-WAY CONVERSATION – Mark 14:32-42.

In his challenging hour, Yeshua took Peter, James, and John with him and asked them to pray. The key here is that Yeshua asked our Father for direction and to be released from his assignment to die.

Prayer helped Yeshua to place the will of our Father above his own will.

The scripture does not tell us he heard an answer, but it does tell us he refocused to complete his mission. Prayer is not to force our Father to do what we want. It is for us to become resolute in what our Father has planned for us to impact humankind.

> *He said, "Abba, Father, for you all things are possible; remove this cup from me, yet not what I want but what you want."*
> Mark 14:36 NRSV

PRAYER IS FOR DIRECTION, CORRECTION, AND PROVISION - Matthew 6:10-12

Prayer is a disciple's most powerful tool. We must guard against self-centered or earthly focused prayers. The foundational purpose of prayer is to understand our Father's plans to have his kingdom come and will be done. This does not mean that our Father will not bless his children. It means we focus on the Kingdom first and always seek our Father's will.

> *"Not everyone who says to me, 'Lord, Lord,' will enter the Kingdom of heaven, but only the one who does the will of my Father in heaven."*
> Matthew 7:21 NRSV

PERSONAL PRAYER:

Every disciple must have a personal prayer routine. Our personal prayers are to flow from our Father's plans, to our wants and needs, then seeking to resolve conflicts to maintain peace in our spiritual community and the world.

Disciples should have at least one prayer a day to focus on these things:
- The things God wants - **<u>Matthew 6:10</u>**
- The things you want - **<u>Matthew 6:11-13</u>**
- How to handle conflicts between these two – **<u>Mark 14:36</u>**

> *"May your Kingdom come. May your will be done on earth as it is in heaven. Matthew 6:10*
> *Give us today our daily bread. …Matthew 6:11*
> *Jesus said to him, "If you are able! All things can be done for the one who believes." Mark 9:23" NRSV*

CORPORATE PRAYER - <u>Acts 4:27- 5:6</u> & <u>Colossians</u> <u>1:9-14:</u>

In the scripture in Acts, the community of disciples prayed for boldness, not just for the leaders but for the entire community. Peter stood in this boldness by refusing to allow Ananias and Sapphira to pollute the community with their dishonesty. In the scripture in Colossians, Paul expresses his prayerful desire for the community of disciples in Colossae. His prayer is for the entire community of disciples.

Disciples should have at least one prayer a day for their community of disciples to live and grow in our Father's will.

> "Both Herod and Pontius Pilate, with the gentiles and the peoples of Israel, gathered together against your holy servant[a] Jesus, whom you anointed," Acts 4:27
> "The young men came and wrapped up his body, then carried him out and buried him." Acts 5:6 NRSV

> "For this reason, since the day we heard it, we have not ceased praying for you and asking that you may be filled with the knowledge of God's will in all spiritual wisdom and understanding" Colossians 1:9 NRSV

PRAY BECAUSE YOU ARE NEVER ALONE - <u>Psalm 23</u>

Each stanza of this psalm reassures disciples that our Father is a caring and protective shepherd. Regardless of what we experience, He is our shepherd; therefore, we will not lack.

We must live as sheep surrendered and committed to his Kingdom will.

> *"Even though I walk through the darkest valley,
> I fear no evil, for you are with me; your rod and your staff, they comfort me."* Psalm 23:4 NRSV

PRAYER MUST INCLUDE AND SEEK FAITH, HOPE, AND LOVE: <u>1 Corinthians 13</u>

Paul teaches the disciples in Corinth that spiritual *Gifts* are great, but they mean nothing without exemplifying the character of a disciple.

Our prayers must include Faith in our Father, hope for the world, and love for each other.

Always have these three as the focus of our prayers:

FAITH * HOPE * LOVE

> *"And now faith, hope, and love remain, these three, and the greatest of these is love."* 1 Corinthians 13:13 NRSV

PRAYER TO IMPACT PEOPLE FOR THE KINGDOM OF GOD – <u>Matthew 9:9-13:</u>

Our mission as disciples is to introduce sinners to the Savior, Yeshua the Christ. While some will treat the community as an exclusive club, disciples pray daily for opportunities to make New Disciples. Always pray to impact the lost with an invitation to become a disciple of Yeshua.

> *"I have not come to call the righteous but Sinners to repentance."* Luke 5:32 NRSV

NOTES

EARLY DISCIPLE DEVELOPMENT
(Spiritual Age is 2 – 5 years)

"Observation, Assisting, & Developing Language…Key Tools for Young Disciples."

The new disciple has been saved for 2 – 3 years. This is the stage where the disciple starts to assist others in ministry. In assisting, observing how scripture is implemented in the life of a disciple is vital. Observation is a key tool for young disciples.

The examples and information received during this stage will strengthen the focus of the young disciple.

In addition to observation, the young disciple should start learning how to understand scripture. Good study habits must be developed in this stage. Because observation is a key component in this stage, the young disciple should be involved in a study group at least once a week. This will allow the young disciple to observe how mature disciples study the word. The young disciples should not be challenged to interpret scripture;

they are learning how to study scripture. Bible Study is not a study group. A study group comes together to leverage tools (e.g. commentaries, books, articles) to understand what a scripture means.

The investment in prayer must steadily increase. The young disciple should start developing spiritual language as a habit. Calling on the Lord should become second nature. This will allow the young disciple to unconsciously remember God and their Kingdom commitment. In this stage, the young disciple knows that they are a child of God and that God will always love them and keep them in righteousness. The young disciple develops confidence in their relationship with the loving God.

MINISTRY LEVEL

The young disciple must start to demonstrate reliability and responsibility. They are not supervised closely. Correction is still very important.

They must demonstrate accountability for their actions. This is a good time to allow the young disciple to assist in ministry.

They should experience the work needed to do ministry. For example, they should assist by making sandwiches for mission activities and setting up classes and events. They must see these opportunities as a privilege because of the growth they have demonstrated by understanding that they are first mimicking the mature disciples in the community.

They must be exposed to good leadership and learn what it means to invest in doing the work for successful ministry outcomes.

Outline
Understanding How to Help

- Every disciple must be willing to be an effective helper to the community and/or leadership.
- You cannot lead until you are able and willing to help.

What is the *Gift/Ministry of Helps*? - The basic difference between the *Gift of Helps* and the *Ministry of Helps* is that one is gifted (compelled) to assist and the other does so out of kindness. A person with the Gift or Ministry of Helps is someone who tends to work behind the scenes to get things done. The individual with this gift will often do his/her job joyfully and take the responsibilities off others' shoulders.

They have a personality that is humble and have no problem sacrificing time and energy to do God's work. They even have an ability to see what others need often before they even know they need it.

People with this spiritual gift have a great attention to detail and tend to be very loyal. They often go above and beyond in everything and are often described as having a servant's heart.

People in the Bible Who Helped God's People

- *ATTITUDE OF DISCIPLES* - <u>**Matthew 5:1-16.**</u>
  This scripture is to teach disciples to be selfless. Verses 1-12 teach the attitude disciples must surrender into.

  Becoming Selfless

  Verses 13-16 teach disciples to remain 'salt and light.' Disciples are to impact the world as a way of life.

> *"In the same way, let your light shine before others, so that they may see your good works and give glory to your Father in heaven."*
> Matthew 5: 16 NRSV

- *RAHAB* – <u>Joshua 2:1-14</u> & <u>Matthew 1:5.</u>

Rahab is not a likely candidate to bless God's people. Some would frown on her because of her profession. However, she chose to side with Yahweh and protect the spies. In return, she requested protection for her family and everyone connected to them when Israel invaded Jericho.

Rahab became a citizen of Israel and married Salmon. She was the mother of Boaz, which means she was David's great-grandmother, and in the lineage of Yeshua.

But the woman took the two men and hid them.[a] Then she said, "True, the men came to me, but I did not know where they came from…." Joshua 2:4 NRSV

- *HELPING DISCIPLES* – <u>Matthew 24:36-25:46</u>

This teaching is typically generalized to focus on caring for the less fortunate, but the context is intended to teach disciples to care for each other.

Caring for each other is a priority.

It is fine to care for the less fortunate, but disciples are to care for other disciples first.

> *"For it is as if a man, going on a journey, summoned his slaves and entrusted his property to them."*
> *Matthew 25:14*
> NRSV

- **BEING A COMMUNITY - <u>Acts 4:34.</u>**

    The Holy Spirit *led* disciples to sell their possessions to meet the needs of their spiritual community. Disciples are to care for other disciples first.

- *STEPHEN, PHILIP, PROCHORUS, NICANOR, TIMON, PARMENAS, AND NICOLAUS* - <u>Acts 6:1-6.</u>

    The apostles instructed the community of disciples to select the most mature seven to manage the food distribution so that every disciple would be treated the same regardless of their ethnic origins.

    Equity towards Ethnic Diversity

    > *Therefore, brothers and sisters, select from among yourselves seven men of good standing, full of the Spirit and of wisdom, whom we may appoint to this task," Acts 6:3* NRSV

People in the Bible Who Helped Leaders

SOME DISCIPLES ARE COMMISSIONED TO ASSIST LEADERS

- *JOSHUA* – <u>Exodus 33:7-11</u> & <u>Deuteronomy 31.</u>

    Before Joshua became the leader of Israel, he served Moses. In verse 11, we learn that Joshua would remain in the presence of Yahweh when Moses had to attend to other things. Joshua served Moses, but he did not neglect his preparation to become a leader.

    Learning how to serve Leaders

    Even David served Saul after David had been anointed to be king. Disciples must learn how to serve leaders until Yahweh says to change leaders. Joshua waited until Yahweh told Moses to position Joshua as the next leader (Deuteronomy 31).

> *"The LORD used to speak to Moses face to face, as one speaks to a friend. Then he would return to the camp, but his young assistant, Joshua son of Nun, would not leave the tent." Exodus 33:11 NRSV*

- ### *AARON AND HUR* – <u>Exodus 17:12-13.</u>

    For Israel to win the battle, Moses' arms had to remain raised. When Moses became tired, Aaron and Hur assisted him in keeping his arms raised.

    > *Disciples must learn to be*
    > *in position to carry the*
    > *weight*
    > *when the leader is tired.*

> *"But Moses's hands grew heavy, so they took a stone and put it under him, and he sat on it.*
> *Aaron and Hur held up his hands, one on either side, so his hands were steady until the sun set.*
> *And Joshua defeated Amalek and his people with the sword."*
> *Exodus 17: 12-13 NRSV*

- *JONATHAN* – <u>1 Samuel 23:15-18</u>

    The son of the king is the heir apparent to the throne, next in line to become king. Jonathan loved David and honored Yahweh to the point that he relinquished his right to be king because that was not Yahweh's plan. Jonathan assisted David even when this was against Saul's orders. Disciples must be committed to Yahweh's leaders.

- *AHIMELECH THE PRIEST* – <u>1 Samuel 21:1-6</u>

    When David comes looking for food, the priest Ahimelech only has the holy bread that is reserved for those who have kept themselves from women.

    > *The best of the disciplined and mature disciples still serve leaders.*

    David assures the priest that his men keep themselves from women whenever they are away from home.

    Ahimelech gives David the bread that he needs.

> "David answered the priest, "Indeed, women have been kept from us as always when I go on an expedition; the vessels of the young men are holy even when it is a common journey; how much more today will their vessels be holy?"
> 1 Samuel 21:5 NRSV

- *ELISHA* – <u>**1 Kings 19.**</u>

    Elijah has been instructed to position a king for the northern and southern Kingdoms of Israel and to position his replacement as prophet of Israel. When Elijah throws his mantle on Elisha, he requests to say good-bye to his parents.

We have free will to serve leaders.

Elijah does not instruct him either way because Elisha must make this commitment on his own. He cannot say Elijah told me to do this or that. He commits himself because he knows this mantle is for him. He serves Elijah and learns from him until Yahweh decides to make a switch.

> "He left the oxen, ran after Elijah, and said, "Let me kiss my father and my mother, and then I will follow you." Then Elijah[a] said to him, "Go back again, for what have I done to you? "He returned from following him, took the yoke of oxen, and slaughtered them; using the equipment from the oxen, he boiled their flesh and gave it to the people, and they ate. Then he set out and followed Elijah and became his servant. 1 Kings 19: 20-21 NRSV

- *GEHAZI* – **2 Kings 5:15-27.**

    Every assistant is not obedient. Gehazi is selfish and thinks his methods are better than the prophet's. He thinks he can deceive the prophet who hears from Yahweh.

Disciples must respect instructions even when the instructions are not understood as long as the instructions come from a leader humbly following Yahweh.

JOHN THE BAPTIZER – **John 1:19-42.**

John the baptizer had a thriving ministry; however, he understood his *Calling*. He was commissioned to prepare the way for Yeshua. When John exclaimed, "here is the Lamb of

God," two of his disciples heard this and followed Yeshua.

Some disciples are commissioned to prepare the way for someone else; to help build and develop their ministry.

John's ministry was to release those who followed him to follow Yeshua. This is not just working behind the scenes. This is building a ministry to transfer to someone else.

> *"May the LORD pardon your servant on one count: when my master goes into the house of Rimmon to worship there, leaning on my arm, and I bow down in the house of Rimmon, when I do bow down in the house of Rimmon, may the LORD pardon your servant on this one count." 2 Kings 5:18 NRSV*

- *BARNABAS* – <u>Acts 4:32-5:6</u>, <u>Acts 9:26-30</u>, <u>Acts 11:19-26</u>, <u>Acts 13:1- 3</u>, Acts 14:1 and <u>Acts 14:14.</u>

  Barnabas is a powerful example of being obedient to leaders and assisting leaders. He does what he is instructed to do. He invested in

Paul and was set aside with Paul to become an apostle.

*His willingness to serve and obey
led to his consecration as an apostle.*

> *"But Barnabas took him, brought him to the apostles, and described for them how on the road he had seen the Lord, who had spoken to him, and how in Damascus, he had spoken boldly in the name of Jesus."* Acts 9:27 NRSV

- *SILAS* – **Acts 15:36-41**, **Acts 16:16-40.**

    Paul selects Silas to be his assistant when Silas is about to return home. Silas was sent with Paul by the apostles in Jerusalem to deliver a message to the Jews. He was intending to return home. When Paul selects him to travel with him, he respects this positioning. He is faithful and supportive. Paul is never frustrated by Silas.

NOTES

MIDDLE DISCIPLE DEVELOPMENT
(Spiritual Age is 6 – 12 years)

"This is the stage where the young disciple must start to demonstrate the ability and willingness to make sound spiritual decisions."

The young disciple has been saved for 4–5 years. There is a direct investment in learning and demonstrating sound decision-making skills. The young disciples should be challenged to demonstrate that they can follow the teachings of Yeshua through the decisions and choices they make. They must be supervised, but they must also demonstrate that they are fulfilled and energized to be a disciple of Yeshua the Christ.

The young disciple is not ready for leadership, but they should be a reliable team member or volunteer.

They should demonstrate a willingness to be engaged in the work of ministry without much prompting. If the young disciple is unwilling or unable to demonstrate the heart and passion for the things of God, then they must spend more time in *Early Disciple Development* being exposed to good leadership, so they understand what it means to invest in doing the work for successful ministry outcomes. It is important that the young disciple not progress to the *Middle Disciple Development* phase until they have demonstrated the ministry level at the prior phase. This *Middle Disciple Development* stage is where the young disciple demonstrates their love for God and their commitment to be a good steward in all aspects of life without prompting.

> *This Middle Disciple Development stage is where the young disciple demonstrates their love for God and their commitment to be a good steward in all aspects of life without prompting.*

MINISTRY LEVEL

For the most part, there can be an increase in responsibility for the young disciple, but there should be little to no change in their level of ministry involvement.

Outline

We will learn how to be good stewards of our resources by studying *My Giving Strategy*.

My Giving Strategy

Many believers miss the power and privilege of giving because we do not plan to give. Additionally, the Bible teaches that giving is a spiritual gift. Giving has always been a significant component of worship. In the First Covenant (Old Testament), the offering was the first expression of worship. This standard continues in the Second Covenant (New Testament) in that believers are to surrender themselves to God as the first offering of worship.

Worship is not a series of actions; it is a series of offerings. Every aspect of worship can and should be understood in the context of offering. Little, if anything, in our worship should be focused on us. Worship is our opportunity to honor God for all God has been and continues to be to us. Therefore, believers must invest in transforming how we understand and participate in worship. Our worship must satisfy God, not ourselves.

This information is based on my book entitled *Cheerfully*. The intention of this stage is to aid you in developing your giving strategy. The goal is to become a giver *led* by the Holy Spirit for every offering you release as you become a sacrificial giver.

It is my prayer that you grow through this information and that you give to express your love for God, not just to meet financial needs. Giving is the only way that we can display our love for God.

This statement is not just focused on financial giving. Everything we give to God must be considered an offering and must be spotless and sincere.

Giving is a Gift of the Spirit

To approach the task of developing a giving strategy, I suggest that you first wrestle with your view and understanding of giving. I understand that the church has financial responsibilities, but the act of giving is relational. Obligation can take the love out of the act. For example, as a child, would you have preferred that your parents fed you out of obligation (because they had to) or out of love (because they wanted to)? The act of obligation may exist, but it cannot be the motivation for giving. As children of God, we must understand that God wants our love and attention, not out of obligation but out of a profound desire to please our God.

*Giving can never be an obligation
if it is going to be an expression of
love and worship*

Romans 12:3-8 offers an opportunity to help us reframe our view and understanding of giving. Giving is not just an act of worship; for some, it is a gift of the Spirit.

We have not invested much focus in understanding this gift; therefore, there is a wide range of opinions on how this gift is to operate in the body of Christ.

> *[3]For by the grace given to me I say to everyone among you not to think of yourself more highly than you ought to think, but to think with sober judgment, each according to the measure of faith that God has assigned. [4]For as in one body we have many members, and not all the members have the same function, [5]so we, who are many, are one body in Christ, and individually we are members one of another. [6]We have gifts that differ according to the grace given to us: prophecy, in proportion to faith; [7]ministry, in ministering; the teacher, in teaching; [8]the exhorter, in exhortation; the giver, in generosity; the leader, in diligence; the compassionate, in cheerfulness.* NRSV

Romans 12:3 instructs us to humbly consider our role in the body with sober judgment. There are two competing approaches, and both must be defeated for us to sincerely perceive the *Gifts* that God has assigned to us. Some think too highly of themselves, causing them to aspire for the *Gifts* they view as important, conveying significance and authority to a few. This approach clouds our understanding of our *Gifts* because we assign importance to some *Gifts* over others. All *Gifts* of the Spirit have equal significance and importance to the body. Others have no regard for themselves, thinking they are so insignificant that God could not desire to do anything of importance through them. Both opposing views must be defeated for each of us to simply be who God has designed us to be.

Paul says the significant element in understanding our *Gifts* is "the measure of faith that God has assigned." What does this mean? Every gift comes with a measure of faith that is needed to execute the gift. The believer must believe by faith that God has equipped them to be effective and impactful through their gift. If you do not access the measure of faith to execute in your gift, you will never experience the fullness of what God has positioned you for. Your church community will never benefit from your association.

Each of us has been positioned in a church community for two reasons:

- To receive from the ministry so we can grow to assist the vision and mission of that community.
- To offer ourselves to participation in the vision and mission of the community. Therefore, it is imperative for each of us to seek out our *Gifts* so that we can be invested in and sacrifice to serve through our *Gifts*.

In this list of spiritual *Gifts* Paul mentions "the giver, in generosity." One of the key reasons that the gift of giving is not flowing through the church is that givers must be protected. People with the gift of giving are driven by generosity. They must be protected from everyone who will exploit their gift in the church and outside of the church. There are so many greedy and selfish people serving in the church that the giver can be exploited by the teachings and actions of the church. Therefore, developing a giving strategy is important. It eliminates responding to prompting for giving. A strategy prepares for giving before entering corporate worship.

It also removes the need for prompting in worship because the believers come ready to give in spirit and substance. So many people with the gift of giving have been exploited and defeated by people in the church who did not know how to honor and protect this gift. We must invest in an appropriate environment for the gift of giving to be manifested and respected.

Can you see God gifting people to give just as people are gifted to lead and prophesy? Can you embrace giving as a gift of the spirit? This is not an assertion that you have the gift of giving. However, it is necessary for you to understand giving beyond the offering moment in worship if you are going to honestly develop and execute your giving strategy. Just as every believer is asked to show mercy and evangelize.

Every believer is asked to give. While showing mercy, evangelizing, and giving, these *Gifts* of the spirit are to be part of the lifestyle and activity of every believer.

Why is a Giving Strategy Necessary?

To fully understand the concept of giving and the strategy that is birthed from it, reading *Cheerfully* is necessary. There is misinformation and misunderstanding about giving. The church has focused on the amount of the offering and the need for financial resources instead of investing in the biblical importance of giving. In short, we give to express our love and thanksgiving to God. This is the only motivation that will allow an offering to be received by God as worship.

God does not want 'Giving' to cause a financial strain or to generate any form of frustration. God does not desire for believers to have to be convinced to give or for giving to be the sole reason for believers coming together. The church needs to equip the saints for the work of ministry and reach the world with the Gospel. There is no time or place for functions, activities, or programs that are solely to raise money.

Giving must be thoughtful, generous, and strategic. Imagine an offering plea in the Temple. The priest says, "God needs 100 people to give 50 sheep right now. Who has enough faith to trust God and release 50 sheep?" This would not be practical or appropriate. The people determined the offering they would bring based on what God had already instructed and what was in their hearts to give to God.

We have allowed giving to drive people away from the church and for the offering to become more important than the *Word* and worship. Developing a giving strategy will reverse all of these conditions. As the church moves to understand giving as an expression of worship that reflects our love for God, many of the obstacles that have prevented so many from embracing Yeshua and others from focusing on their *Gifts* and *Callings* will be destroyed.

A giving strategy will allow giving to become a part of our lifestyle, not just a part of the worship service. Many believers only consider giving when they are in a worship service. Giving is intended to be a lifestyle that is motivated by love and thankfulness. The way we understand and practice giving has stripped the act of giving of its importance as an expression to God from the giver.

The Bible contains standards for giving. Many of us struggle to achieve these standards because we do not plan to give. Giving has become an impulse or a reaction based on our financial condition. This has caused inconsistent giving, while God intended for giving to be as normal and consistent as singing a song in worship. Investing time to teach giving and assisting people to develop a giving

strategy will reframe giving and increase the willingness of believers to give. I encourage you to invest in developing your giving strategy and execute it out of love and thanksgiving to God, not obligation to the church.

Phase 1
Systematic Giving

The key to an effective giving strategy is consistency. We cannot become consistent in giving if the objective is more than we can afford. Many people teach and believe that a tenth is the optimal level of giving. This will be addressed later, but at this time, it is necessary to understand that the first element of an effective giving strategy is to be honest about what you can afford and honest about what you desire to give.

Our first step is to frame our understanding of giving based on a percentage instead of the amount. We must be able to remove any external motivation or pressure and simply execute our strategy. In Phase One, we will not think about faith or sacrifice. Phase One is based solely on what you can afford.

For those who have made it beyond this phase, do not retreat; move to Phase Two, Three, or Four, depending on where you are in your giving. Phase One is for the believer who is inconsistent in giving or unable to see how they can give at least ten percent based on their financial situation.

- Develop a comprehensive budget: Before we can consider what to give to God, we must have a clear and honest picture of our financial condition and responsibilities. A budget must be documented in a software tool or on paper. A budget that is only in your mind changes every time you change your mind. If you are going to become disciplined to give to God what God deserves, you must be willing to gain control of your financial situation. An unwillingness to develop financial discipline is telling God, "I do not want to get to a position where I can consistently express my love and thanksgiving through my offering." To develop a comprehensive budget, you must record every financial transaction that you have. I suggest that you only use a debit card for 30 days. It will allow all of your transactions to be recorded in your bank account. Then you will have a clear picture of what you spend on movies, gum, and eating at restaurants.

Many of us may find that we cannot afford to give anything to God. This is where your first decision needs to be made. What are you willing to cut or stop doing to make room for giving? Are you willing to eat at home

one additional day a week to free up ten to twenty dollars? Are you willing to cut back on shopping or something else to make room to give?

- Once you have decided what you can afford to give, turn this amount into a percentage of your total income, including all sources of income. Don't commit to giving God a specific amount. Commit to giving God a percentage. It is important to build your strategy on percentages because this will allow you to be consistent regardless of your income. In this phase, your commitment is to give to God a consistent percentage out of everything received. Even if you receive money for your birthday, you will give the percentage to God because you love God.

- This phase is for those who cannot or are not willing to give a tenth. Phase 1 is for the giver who is giving less than ten percent. If your giving percentage is at ten percent or greater, move to phase 2 or 3.

- Once you have given **consistently** at your percentage for 30 days, start developing benchmarks that will progress your giving towards ten percent. You can make incremental decisions to increase your giving as you display more discipline over your spending and continue to reframe your

  understanding of giving based on what you are learning in *Cheerfully*.

- You will graduate from Phase 1 when you are a consistent giver, and your giving percentage becomes ten percent. Remember, the key in phase 1 is to be a consistent giver. Don't feel pressured to rush to a percentage that you cannot afford. Be disciplined in controlling spending and expenses so that you can consciously see the money that you will give to God.

Phase 2
A Tenth as My Minimum

It is important to understand the process of tithing in the first covenant. There are three tithes in the seven-year cycle of giving.

- Giving in the first covenant was executed on a seven-year cycle. The seventh year is the Sabbath Year, and the seventh cycle of seven years (49) is the year of Jubilee, the Sabbath of Sabbaths. In Jubilee, there is a national reset: debt is removed, land is returned, etc.
- Once you arrive at giving ten percent, you must invest in making this consistent. In phase 2, you will document the times that you do not give ten percent. You should have developed consistency in phase 1; therefore, the percentage objective of your giving should not impact your consistency. The objective of phase 2 is to understand the tenth in two ways:

    In *Cheerfully*, I assert that giving a tenth based on the law is a flawed understanding of God and the law. The tenth is significant because it was the standard that Abraham and Jacob gave to God before the law. In the law, God defined the tenth as the minimum expression of love. In this phase, dispel the understanding that you must give a tenth. This is restrictive thinking and will prevent you from understanding giving in the time of grace. We will be in the time of grace until Yeshua returns. Understand the tenth as a standard used by Abraham, Jacob, and God, but not as an obligation. The tenth is not a magical percentage that will open blessings or windows of heaven. It is a standard of love that was established to inform us of God's expectation of our love and faith.

- Understand the tenth as your minimum. The tenth has been so emphasized that many of us are unable to hear God's desire for us to go further. Poor stewardship and misinformed teaching have caused some to believe that arriving at giving a tenth is the pinnacle of giving. This is not true. Yeshua came with a new standard for giving, and the Holy Spirit opened this standard to the believers in the book of *The Acts of the Apostles*. To transition to phase 3, you must see the tenth as the minimum percentage that you will ever give to God going forward.

- The overemphasis of the tenth has caused many givers to be constrained to a law that does not allow us to experience giving in the context that Yeshua offers in his life and ministry. This overemphasis has especially impacted the gift of giving because those gifted to give do not experience the opportunity to obey God at new levels. Many gifted givers have turned to charities and good causes for their giving above ten percent because the church has not taught the standard of giving that Yeshua ushered into the life of the disciples.

I do not have an issue with giving to charities and good causes, but givers, especially gifted givers, must consult with God to know where to release their resources. The church community is the repository for the offerings that believers release. The church community then engages in ministry to display the love of God to the world.

If you do not believe that your church community will be good stewards of your offerings, then you must address this. You will not faithfully execute your giving strategy if you do not believe or trust those who are responsible for managing the financial gifts. You cannot hesitate or refuse to address this concern. God wants to liberate our giving in two more phases; this cannot happen if there is any reservation about the stewardship of your church community..

Your church community must adhere to the standards of the Internal Revenue Service or the governing body of your country and fully comply with the Bible. Therefore, it is important for your stewardship leaders to read *Cheerfully* and lead your church community in implementing a clear biblical understanding of giving as an expression of worship in love and thanksgiving. For you and your church community to be liberated by the teachings of Yeshua and the power of the Holy Spirit, you must be willing to share your thoughts and feelings if you do not have confidence in the management of your stewardship leaders.

Phase 3
Giving *'Led'* by the Holy Spirit

To receive direction from the Holy Spirit, we must desire to give to God according to God's desire for us. This is when we become Worship Givers. A Worship Giver releases an offering as part of their corporate worship above ten percent. In phases One and Two, we were focused on what we could afford and the standards of Abraham, Jacob, and God (legal). Now, we can experience liberation in our giving. We can be *led* by the Holy Spirit in our regular giving.

It is important to remember that the Holy Spirit will never lead us to give less than a tenth. It is important to understand the difference between the guidance of the Holy Spirit and the disciplined decisions that we may need to make because of changes in our financial situation. Therefore, we did not use faith or sacrifice in phases One and

Two. These principles will be key in phases Three and Four.

The biblical information we have on giving *led* by the Holy Spirit is found in chapters 4 and 5 of the book of *The Acts of the Apostles. In Acts 2:44-45 and Acts 4:32-33,* we are informed that the disciples released personal possessions for the benefit of the community (church) based on the 'leading' of the Holy Spirit. We will focus on the events of Acts 4:31 – 5:, 6. The information leading to the events of Joseph of Cyprus and the transition from Joseph to Ananias and Sapphira are important to understand giving *led* by the Holy Spirit.

Acts 4:31 informs us that these disciples have been filled with the Holy Spirit. It is not clear if this is a different group of disciples from the group in Acts 2:1-11. However, I do not think this is the point of this information. I think the author wants to ensure that we readers know the actions that happen next are *led* by the Holy Spirit.

The remainder of Acts 4 informs us that these disciples did the following things after being filled with the Holy Spirit:

- They were of one heart and soul – this reflects their level of unity and agreement. They were not motivated to invest in individualism but by mutual respect and a focus on their common agreement in Yeshua. They were not trying to preserve or protect themselves; their concern and focus were for the community of disciples. This does not mean they acted and thought the same, but it does mean everything they thought and did was for the well-being of the community of disciples above and beyond themselves.
- They held their private possessions in common – this does not mean they sold all of their possessions. It means they did not hold anything back from consideration to meet the needs of the community of disciples. Ownership of a thing or how important that thing was to the person did not matter. They

were *led* by the Holy Spirit to consider the community of disciples beyond themselves. Anything they owned could be sold to meet the needs of the community of disciples.

- The Apostles (leadership) did not focus on the needs of the community of disciples. Their focus was on the sharing and teaching of the Gospel. Many leaders must address operational issues instead of focusing on the extension of the vision of the community of disciples and the Gospel of Yeshua. Spiritual Leaders must be allowed to focus on sharing the Resurrection and demonstrating the reality of God through great power.

  If there was a need in the community, the Holy Spirit led some to sell things to meet the need. There were no needy in the community of disciples because they allowed the Holy Spirit to lead them to release what they had to care for each other. Laying the money at the Apostles' feet was a sign of dependence. It indicated that they were dependent on the

Apostles to ensure their needs were met. This was very different from an offering. This was a demonstration of dependence.

- Acts 4 ends with information about a person named Joseph of Cyprus who not only sold a field but also relinquished his identity by embracing his new name, and in doing so, he embraced the purpose the Apostles saw for him. Joseph is discussed so that we understand why the actions of Ananias and Sapphira are so egregious.

- Ananias appears to do the same thing that Joseph of Cyprus did, but Peter asked him, "Why has Satan filled your heart to lie to the Holy Spirit and to keep back part of the proceeds of the land?"

- Ananias and Sapphira teach us never to misrepresent what we give and always to be honest in every aspect of worship.

- Peter shows spiritual leaders that we must be in tune with the Holy Spirit to address any act that is counterfeit and thus ungodly.

- Spiritual leaders can never become so concerned about the offering that they do not protect the integrity of the community of disciples. Ananias and Sapphira died because their mindset could not be allowed to live. The integrity of the community is so important that the Holy Spirit wanted everyone to know this behavior will not be allowed. Note – they do not die under the law; they die in the age of grace. The Holy Spirit placed the integrity of the community above giving them an opportunity to be restored. The Holy Spirit made them an example for all of us to learn from.

The standard of giving exemplified and taught by Yeshua is to, "Surrender all that I am and have to God." Just as Yeshua gave himself for our redemption, we are called to surrender everything we are and must be *led* by the Holy Spirit.
The liberty of this phase is that we seek the Holy Spirit to know what God desires from us in every

aspect of life, including our giving. In this phase, we are seeking to receive our percentage from the Holy Spirit. Some in Acts gave everything and laid the proceeds at the Apostles' feet. What is the Holy Spirit leading you to release?

This release is not based on what you can afford. It must be an act of faith to trust God and do whatever the Holy Spirit is leading you to release. This is not based on an offering plea. This is your

new level of consistent giving until the Holy Spirit leads you to do something different. Remember, the Holy Spirit will never lead you to give less than ten percent.

Phase 4
Sacrificial Giving

Sacrificial Giving is temporary offerings that are in addition to what the Holy Spirit has *led* you to give. This level of giving can be executed in two conditions:

- By instruction from the Holy Spirit – the Holy Spirit can prompt you to add to your regular offering as a demonstration of your growing trust and faith in God. You do not inform anyone of this. You do what the Holy Spirit is instructing. This giving does not impact your consistent percentage, but it is in addition to the percentage you have been *led* to give by the Holy Spirit.

  By direction from your spiritual leader – at this level, you should not be open to exploitation because you have invested in knowing how the Holy Spirit is leading you. You have also invested in trusting your church community through open and continuous dialogue. You are now ready to respond to needs that are presented by your spiritual leader.

- There is a component of sacrificial giving that we did not discuss in the other phases, but it should be applied in phase 1. Having an investment strategy is very important for your giving strategy. Believers should know how to benefit from informed conservative investing. The historical rate of return of the stock market is ten percent, which is far better than any savings account or mutual fund. The issue with investing is that it requires time and study.

- Investing is key to your giving strategy because the earnings can supplement your offerings, especially in Sacrificial Giving. To give in addition to what the Holy Spirit has *led* you to give will require having access to additional income. Some get a part-time job temporarily to have a sacrificial gift. For some, this is fine. However, as a standard practice, believers should be improving their stewardship by demonstrating they can generate increase from what they have been given. This principle is evident in Matthew 25:14-30 and Luke 19:11-27. While these texts do not tell us how the good stewards generated the increase, it does tell us that they generated an increase. In Matthew, Yeshua tells the last servant that you could have at least put it in the bank and received interest.

Sacrificial Giving will be based on your willingness to be a disciplined steward of what God has given you and how you manage it. Investing is not a vehicle to gamble with our resources. Markets are volatile; consequently, you can lose money investing. We should seek to implement some form of investment strategy so that the increase can be shared with God.

- Sacrificial Giving is a privilege and a necessary part of giving. Before considering any ministry or good cause outside of your church community, always consider giving to your church. Always listen to *your* spiritual leader before you listen to a spiritual leader.

It is my prayer that your spiritual leader can hear God speaking truth in this material. I pray that you hear God addressing the struggles and concerns you may have had with giving, especially to those gifted givers. I pray that you are liberated in a safe environment to give under the protection of God, the Holy Spirit, and prudent spiritual leadership that will ensure you are not exploited because of your gift.

My Giving Strategy Worksheet

Phase 1

Systematic Giving

The key to an effective giving strategy is consistency. If you are not currently giving at the level of ten percent this phase is to assist you to develop consistency in percentage-based giving. Based on your budget, determine the percentage you will give based on your pay cycle.

I vow to give _____% every _____ starting _____.

My plan is to increase to give _____% every _____ starting _____.

My plan is to increase to give _____% every _____ starting _____.

My plan is to increase to give _____% every _____ starting _____.

My plan is to increase to give _____% every _____ starting _____.

Phase 2

A tenth as my minimum

Once I arrive at giving ten percent, I must display consistency in giving at this level. To display my consistency, I vow to give ten percent consistently starting on _____.

I will also document the times I give less than ten percent to recognize my inconsistency:

✓ I did not give ten percent as my minimum on _____.

✓ I did not give ten percent as my minimum on _____.

✓ I did not give ten percent as my minimum on _____.

✓ I did not give ten percent as my minimum on _____.

Phase 3

Giving *led* by the Holy Spirit.

To receive direction from the Holy Spirit I must desire to give to God according to God's desire for me. This is when I become a Worship Giver.

I vow to seek the Holy Spirit for the percentage I am to give above ten percent starting on

_____.

The Holy Spirit has instructed me to start giving _____% starting on _____.

I vow to consistently give this percentage.

As a cheerful giver, Yahweh has given me the following increase:

_____
_____
_____
_____
_____

Phase 4

Sacrificial Giving

This is where my good stewardship and deep love for God can work in conjunction to express my love and thanksgiving to God.

I vow to save and invest to produce a **gift to God from my heart**, as well as position myself to **respond to the sacrificial request** of my spiritual community and to **pour into those that God leads me to support** starting on _____.

This is my Giving Strategy. I affix my signature to this document to hold myself accountable to my vows.

_____

Date: _____

NOTES

ADOLESCENT DISCIPLE DEVELOPMENT

(Spiritual Age is 13 – 20 years)

"The Adolescent Disciple should be fully aware that they are being prepared to lead."

The young disciple has been saved for 6 – 7 years. Based on the strong demonstration of commitment and focus displayed in the Middle stage, the young disciple is ready to take on the responsibility of caring for others. However, the *Adolescent Disciple* should not yet be given the responsibility to teach younger disciples. Instead, they should focus on caring for the sick and elderly. The *Adolescent Disciple* must demonstrate the willingness to manage their schedule and commitments to execute their responsibility of caring without needing prompting or reminders.

Additionally, the *Adolescent Disciple* should be exposed to spiritual *Gifts* and acts of power through the Holy Spirit, which should also be visible in the community by the mature disciples. At this point, they should have a strong prayer life and be ready to demonstrate *Gifts* and power. An *Adolescent Disciple* can be trusted with some limited leadership responsibility, keeping in mind that they are still at an impactful stage of development.

However, they are still in the process of being trained, so they must be supervised and held accountable for their choices and decisions.

MINISTRY LEVEL

The *Adolescent Disciple* can be trusted to function independently but needs consistent supervision. There should be scheduled supervision so that the *Adolescent Disciple* knows that they will be held accountable for their tasks and lifestyle. In partnership with mature disciples, they should visit the sick and elderly to care for them and provide transportation, cleaning, or anything to assist the sick and elderly. They must learn the importance of the spiritual community through their demonstration of care. They must know that the community must care for its members.

Their ministry focus should be demonstrating care.

Outline

Each participant will volunteer to serve in a ministry area within their spiritual community for at least one hour per week for six weeks. Senior Pastors do not need to volunteer but may need to direct participants to a ministry area for volunteering. During your weekly sessions, discuss the volunteer experience and learn how to communicate issues and implement process improvements. To develop into mature disciples, we must learn effective communication within the spiritual community and how to identify and implement process improvements.

Disciples Are Volunteering To Serve

NOTES

Early Adulthood Disciple Development
(Spiritual Age is 21 – 34 years)

"Responsible for demonstrating Christian witness to draw others to Yeshua."

Early Adulthood Disciples serve as leadership assistants. They have demonstrated spiritual strength and commitment. At this stage, they are fully exposed to ministry and the responsibilities of demonstrating Christian witness to draw others to Yeshua. The *Early Adulthood Disciple* needs to learn the essence of leadership and how to manage the responsibility of nurturing other disciples. They can assist *Adult Disciples* (the next development phase) by carrying some of their weight. The *Early Adulthood Disciple* should be eager for their opportunity to lead and make disciples.

With their demonstration of power and commitment, this is the stage where…

- Hunger and thirst are present in zealousness.
- An unquenchable passion for more of God and responsibility in the disciple making community,
are evident.

The Early Adulthood Disciple is held accountable and developed by the Adult Disciple they are assisting.

MINISTRY LEVEL

The *Early Adulthood Disciple* can teach in a controlled environment and may lead at an introductory level, usually under a broader leadership responsibility. They can be subleaders to demonstrate their responsibility. They must evangelize. Now that they have experienced caring for others, it is important for them to merge the power of grace, the Gospel, and the love of God into *Evangelism*. They must experience witnessing to produce a confession of salvation with a commitment to being a disciple and preparing to become a *Disciple Maker*.

This Disciple Must Evangelize

Outline

We will learn methods of *Evangelism* by studying *Disciple Making Evangelism*.

Introduction

Evangelism is both a commission and a *Calling*. The commission of Yeshua in Matthew 28:16-20 applies to all believers. Every follower of Yeshua is commissioned to be a disciple-maker. Some believers are called to reach the world with the love and grace of salvation. This book is for the Commissioned and the Called.

You are Called to *Evangelism* if you have care and compassion for the lost, broken, and hurting. Your caring drives you to desire healing and restoration for people through the love of our Father in Yeshua, our Savior, and Lord.

While the gift of *Evangelism* may seem natural to you, there is preparation needed to be an effective Disciple-Maker. There is a basic strategy you must understand to, "Reap the harvest," our Father has prepared (Luke 10:2).

To be effective in *Evangelism* you must be hungry and thirsty to impact the world with Yeshua. You cannot be divided or uncommitted to his teachings. Yeshua built the church to prepare believers to be the Kingdom of God. Your primary objective is to inform the world of the grace of God and invite everyone to accept this grace through salvation.

To be a Disciple-Maker, the next step is key. Everyone who accepts the love of our Father through Yeshua is a disciple; therefore, in accepting Yeshua as Savior and Lord, we have also committed to learning, living, and sharing his teachings. A Disciple is a student of Yeshua. You cannot do *Evangelism* without making a Disciple. Making Disciples is the objective of *Evangelism*.

My prayer is for you to invest in being passionate by maintaining your hunger and thirst. Stay focused and motivated, knowing that "the harvest is plentiful, but the laborers are few" (Luke 10:2). I am praying to the Lord of the harvest to send laborers. Holy Spirit, reveal through this book what believers need to perform *Disciple Making Evangelism*.

The Great Commission

Now, the eleven disciples went to Galilee, to the mountain to which Yeshua had directed them. When they saw him, they worshipped him; but some doubted. And Yeshua came and said to them, "All authority in heaven and on earth has been given to me. Go therefore and make disciples of all nations, baptizing them in the name of the Father and of the Son and of the Holy Spirit, and teaching them to obey everything that I have commanded you. And remember, I am with you always, to the end of the age."
Matthew 28:16-20 NRSV

Many identify this text as the *Great Commission* because Yeshua is instructing the eleven Apostles on what they are to do as His followers. Not every disciple was convinced during this event. The text says, "They worshiped, but some doubted." This could be the reason Yeshua proclaimed He had all authority in heaven and on earth. Even though they were doubting, they still were under His authority to do what He instructed. This instruction was not optional.

They had already made a commitment to follow Him; subsequently, the time had now come for them to demonstrate their commitment. Everything up to this point was preparation. Now they had to demonstrate whether they had reservations or not. This is not to say they had to go forward. It is to say that if they go forward, there cannot be any uncertainty. They have to confidently represent His teachings and life example.

Their instructions are to make 'Disciples of **all nations.**' **All Nations** means no one is off limits to become a Disciple. There should be no division among His followers, especially based on ethnic differences. Any person can become a Disciple, which is a committed student who agrees to learn, live, and share the teachings they receive – a concept we will further explore. New Disciple trainees are to be baptized and taught to obey everything that the eleven were taught during their preparation. This is not exclusive to just the parables and lessons recorded in scripture. This includes the life lessons and challenges the eleven had to experience in order to be prepared.

In order for the Church to reinstate the importance of The Great Commission, we must first develop a Disciple-producing focus and process. After studying the Gospels and *The Acts of the Apostles*, we have concluded that making disciples requires three components – learn, live, and share. Committed Disciples will understand that we remain in this process of development and sharing continually. Disciples never arrive at a level where they do not need to learn, live, or share the teachings of Yeshua.

It is worth noting this commission was before they were filled with the power of the Holy Spirit, and they did not think they were ready. Yeshua did not solicit their consent for this phase of the mission. Yeshua was adhering to the plan of the Father; consequently, the eleven had to decide if they were going to accept the transition from student to teacher by implementing what they had been taught.

Their preparation did not tell them how to make disciples. Their preparation was loaded with the principles and standards of the Kingdom. They learned the principles. Now they had to live them to demonstrate that these principles and standards were practical and possible. The principles Yeshua taught were forgiveness, marriage, loving your neighbor as yourself, etc. There are many principles and standards that Yeshua taught. This is why the church must invest in preparing disciples in the teachings of Yeshua.

Lastly, they were to share these principles and standards with anyone and everyone to offer them the opportunity to do the same. The promise to be with the eleven reassures them that they will have access to the authority and power Yeshua has received. Through Yeshua, they will be able to accomplish this mission.

An essential point of this commission is that Yeshua instructed His disciples to make disciples. This means that we have to be Disciples in order to make Disciples. This is a key component to restoring the effectiveness of the Church. Many do not know what it means to be or make disciples.

> *"And it was in Antioch that the disciples were first called 'Christians.'"*
> Acts 11:26 NRSV

The general understanding of the term Christian is a follower or believer in Yeshua as the Christ or Messiah. This term should lead us to a commitment to follow the teachings of Yeshua. However, it has become a label that does not yield the discipline and focus that the eleven disciples developed during their preparation.

Only Disciples can make Disciples. This does not mean that followers of Yeshua need to change the term that identifies us from Christians back to Disciples. This means that committed followers of Yeshua must pursue learning, living, and sharing the principles and standards (teachings) of Yeshua. It was never the intention of the Gospel to produce believers. Further, it is clear that Yeshua taught the disciples that productivity was a key criterion for being a Disciple of Yeshua. In Matthew 13:1–23, Mark 4:1–20, Luke 8:4-15, Yeshua taught the *Parable of the Sower*. This parable was so important to Matthew that an explanation of the parable is recorded (vv. 18–23). The lesson of this parable is to inform Disciples how to identify committed Disciples by identifying "good soil."

> *Verse 23 explains 'good soil' – "But as for what was sown on good soil, this is the one who hears the word and understands it, who indeed bears fruit and yields, in one case a hundredfold, in another sixty, and in another thirty."*

Disciples produce more Disciples. A Disciple does not simply believe Yeshua is Lord. Disciples commit to learn, live, and share His teachings. This parable was part of the foundational teaching the eleven disciples received to prepare them for the commission.

Learn means to read, study, memorize, and contextually understand the teachings of Yeshua. This will focus on the Gospels of Matthew, Mark, Luke, and John. In reading and studying the Gospels, it is important to take the journey with the disciples. Sit in the class with them and observe how their lives were reshaped into productive *Disciple Makers*. The lessons and experiences they received were part of the process to make them effective disciples. To learn without the life experiences and struggles the eleven had will develop knowledge without the character and discipline required to be a follower of Yeshua.

Live means to implement what has been learned. Learning the teachings of Yeshua is so that Disciples know how to live and interact with each other and the culture around them. Disciples demonstrate faith and commitment through the life we live. Disciples cannot know the teachings and not attempt to live them. Just as the first disciples failed and struggled at times, this is how they were developed into *Disciple Makers.*

Remember, the eleven did not believe they were ready. While Matthew 28 is a kind of graduation, they did not know graduation was coming. They did not have a set curriculum so that they could see graduation coming. The same must be true for our Disciple Making journey. Disciples must remain open for the Holy Spirit to teach and lead us to new understandings through new experiences.

Share means to seek to identify people who will believe, accept salvation, and consciously commit to learn, live, and share the teachings of Yeshua. Sharing must begin as a result of living the teachings of Yeshua. People must observe the teachings of Yeshua being demonstrated in the behavior and decision-making of Disciples. This does not mean that Disciples will not make mistakes or have struggles. This reality must be used to advance Disciple Making. People must have the opportunity to know that committing to becoming a Disciple does not mean that our issues are resolved, and that we have it all together. It means that we are willing to grow through mistakes and life experiences.

The books of the New Testament after the Gospels of Matthew, Mark, Luke, and John are all part of the disciple-making process. *The Acts of the Apostles* inform us of how the community of disciples implemented the teachings of Yeshua and how they understood disciple-making. The Epistles inform us of how spiritual leaders like Peter, James, and Paul taught and addressed the issues of being disciples and a Disciple-Making community. Revelation informs us of the

reward for a disciple's commitment and the fate for rejecting the opportunity to become a disciple.

Clearly, this commission is great because it frames the ministry that the disciples were to focus on as they proceeded after the ascension. The Church must return to a Disciple-Making focus in order to continue to fulfill this commission of Yeshua. In order for the Church to refocus, it is necessary for you to recommit and refocus. It is important that you decide if you will simply believe in Yeshua as Lord or if you will follow Him. Following Him means learning from Him, living like Him, and sharing Him with the world.

What is Disciple Making Evangelism?

The dictionary defines *Evangelism* as, "The spreading of the Christian gospel by public preaching or personal witness."

This is a good historical definition, but it does not necessarily offer the specifics that Disciples need to understand this term in relation to the commission Yeshua instituted. *Evangelism* is inviting all nations to make a conscious commitment to learn, live, and share the principles and standards Yeshua established.

Making Disciples is not focused on securing a confession to salvation. It is focused on securing a commitment to prepare to become a Disciple Maker.

Evangelism has two phases:

- Soliciting a conscious commitment to learn, live, and share the principles and standards of Yeshua.
- Ensuring this new Disciple trainee receives the teachings (principles and standards) of Yeshua.

Note that there is no mention of accepting Yeshua as their Lord and Savior. Why? Some people may need to learn who Yeshua is before they are ready to consciously receive salvation. When salvation is the primary focus of *Evangelism*, it may not result in making Disciples. The primary focus of *Disciple Making Evangelism* is the conscious commitment to learn, live, and share the teachings of Yeshua.

The world is full of uncommitted, saved people because the focus of *Evangelism* has been to acquire the confession of Yeshua as Lord and Savior. This confession is the beginning of a new life, but this confession without a conscious commitment to becoming a Disciple does not adhere to the Great Commission. Yeshua never once mentioned salvation or the confession to salvation in the Great Commission. The focus and intent of the commission is for people of all nations to become Disciples, not simply to be saved.

The confession of Yeshua as our Lord and Savior is an imperative essential component of being and making Disciples, but it is not a substitute for the commitment to becoming a D*isciple Maker*. Every Disciple must confess Yeshua as the Christ. However, some people may need time and information to make this essential confession.

Disciple Making Evangelism is *Evangelism* that produces a commitment to become a *Disciple Maker*. This does not replace sharing the gospel; it is to complete the gospel message by leading people to a Disciple Making commitment.

One of the difficult realities of *Evangelism* is that everyone is not welcomed in the community of Disciples. Acts 5:1-11 (Ananias and Sapphira) and

8:9-24 (Simon) document that the behavior (intent of the heart) was not in agreement with the standards of the community, so in both cases, the offenders were directly addressed. Every new Disciple must understand that their desires and behaviors cannot be allowed to impact the community negatively.

The objective of *Evangelism* is not to bring anyone into the community of Disciples; it is to bring the committed into the community; therefore, people must be informed of more than just the goodness of Yeshua. They must also be exposed to the expectations of the community. Personal feelings and perspectives cannot be more important than community principles and standards. The health of the community must always outweigh the feelings and desires of the individual.

Evangelists must be well-versed in the standards of the community so that as they interact with potential disciples, they know how to prepare them for the commitment they are being invited to make. *Evangelism* cannot be reduced to confessing Yeshua as Lord and walking away. Evangelists must inform people of the benefits of being a disciple and the cost of this commitment. Evangelists must prepare potential Disciples that the community's well-being is going to be more important than their feelings and preferences. This means that everyone is welcomed, but not everyone will be allowed to join the community of Disciples. Evangelists must protect the integrity and unity of the community over and above the joy of cultivating new Disciples. If the Evangelists do not do this, the spiritual leaders must.

The Obstacles to Successful Evangelism

The greatest obstacle to *Successful Evangelism* is understanding what *Evangelism* is. *Successful*

Evangelism is not based on how many people accept Yeshua as their Savior and Lord. *Successful Evangelism* is about 'leading' people to make a choice. If you want to be an effective evangelist, get in the practice of focusing on the decision (choice). If the person decides they do not want the love and grace of our Father, your *Evangelism* has been successful.

Evangelism is not about convincing people to believe through Yeshua. *Evangelism* is about informing people of the love and grace that is available through Yeshua. Then, offer them the opportunity to receive this love and grace by acknowledging Yeshua as their Savior and Lord.

Many evangelists become overwhelmed and burnt out because they think success is based on how many people accept Yeshua. In Luke 9:5 and 10:10-12, Yeshua prepared the disciples for those who rejected their message:

> *Wherever they do not welcome you, as you are leaving that town shake the dust off your feet as a testimony against them. Luke 9:5 NRSV But whenever you enter a town and they do not welcome you, go out into its streets and say, 'Even the dust of your town that clings to our feet, we wipe off in protest against you. Yet know this: the Kingdom of God has come near.' I tell you, on that day it will be more tolerable for Sodom than for that town. Luke 10: 10-12 NRSV*

Yeshua informed the disciples that there would be people who would not receive the message of love and grace; therefore, you must not solely focus on success based on those who confess Yeshua. Your success lies in effectively sharing the message of love and grace that is offered through Yeshua.

Successful Evangelism also involves knowing what to do once a decision is made. Be prepared for an answer. Never share the love and grace without requesting a decision.

People can accept or reject, but it is your responsibility to lead them to a decision.

- If they accept the love and grace that is in Yeshua, inform them that they are forgiven and have made a commitment to be a Disciple. Their Disciple Making commitment is embedded in their acceptance of the love and grace. Immediately associate them with a Disciple Making community (church) so they can continue learning how to embrace the grace they have received.
- If they reject the love and grace, tell them that you will pray for them to reconsider. Inform them of Matthew 10:32-33. This is not to pressure or frighten them, but to inform them of the impact of their decision. It would be best to share this information before they decide, but ensure they know the impact of their decision. Also, inform them that love and grace through Yeshua are always available to them. Whenever they confess Yeshua as their Savior and Lord, they become a Disciple;

therefore, they will need to become associated with a Disciple Making Community (church).

> *Everyone therefore who acknowledges me before others, I also will acknowledge before my Father in heaven; but whoever denies me before others, I also will deny before my Father in heaven.*
> Matthew 10:32-33 NRSV

Being successful in *Evangelism* requires that you have accepted the love and grace of our Father offered through Yeshua. You do not have to be completely healed or delivered, but you must understand and appreciate the love and grace you have received through salvation.

- Love – Our Father loved the world, so He offered Yeshua on the cross to cover the penalty for sin. Yeshua's death on the cross was not just for those who would believe. His death atoned for all sin, once and for all (Hebrews 10:8-10). The benefits of this love are received by those who are willing to accept them by confessing Yeshua as their

Savior and Lord, then surrendering their lives to learn, live, and share His teachings.

> *When he said above, "You have neither desired nor taken pleasure in sacrifices and offerings and burnt offerings and sin offerings" (these are offered according to the law), then he added, "See, I have come to do your will." He abolishes the first in order to establish the second. And it is by God's will that we have been sanctified through the offering of the body of Jesus Christ once for all.*
> Hebrews 10:8-10 NRSV

- Grace – Our Father is willing to offer sinful people a path to be forgiven and restored to have a loving relationship with Him; this is grace. Grace cannot be earned and will never be deserved. Grace is a choice made by our Father because of love. Our Father is the only one who can offer grace because He is the one who is offended by sin. He is the one who can determine what will satisfy the offense of sin. Our Father decided that Yeshua's obedient surrender on the cross would satisfy the offense of sin. To be forgiven, we need Yeshua to confess us to our Father. Yeshua said he would only confess us if we confessed him to people.

The love of our Father is expressed through grace. The grace of our Father is the evidence (demonstration) of his love.

The Importance of Evangelism in Disciple Making

The commission from Yeshua explicitly states that Disciples are to be produced from all nations. I do not isolate this instruction to merely sharing the gospel in all countries and languages. While this approach is commendable, it sidesteps a key issue the disciples had to address. In the book of *The Acts of the Apostles*, the Church was not merely a physical building or location; it was the community in which the disciples interacted and operated. As a community, they had to learn how to live together, respect, and appreciate one another.

This was a difficult lesson for the disciples to learn and implement. In Acts 6, we are informed that there was an issue between the Jews and the Greeks. The Greeks complained that the Jews were neglecting the needs of Greek widows in the distribution of food. This indicates that the Apostles did not establish separate Jewish and Greek communities. They confronted the ethnic struggles between Jews and Greeks, affirming that the community of disciples would be comprised of individuals from all nations.

Evangelism cannot result in a segregated church; it must be diverse. All people of any condition or station must be welcomed into the community of Disciples. In the current state of the Church, we have found so many ways to be segregated.

We actually promote segregation. Social class and ethnicity are two examples of how we are segregated. They actually say Sunday's are still the most segregated day of the week in America because Whites go to church with Whites, Blacks go to church with Blacks, and the wealthy tend to break bread with the wealthy.

Research shows that people like the idea of diversity, they just don't like being around different people. Maybe their sense of church is the space where they don't have to worry about issues like this.

In Acts 2, the Holy Spirit demonstrated diversity, showing that as we seek unity and agreement, even language will not be a barrier in the community.

The family of God must struggle to undo the myths of separation.

Poor people should not be segregated into separate sections because they are deemed dirty or might steal something. Their marginalized position reflects the church's unwillingness to invest in and share the wealth God has made the community steward over. Also, it is understandable that every ethnicity desires to see themselves reflected in their perceptions of God and Yeshua. However, this concept has been taken too far. Yeshua was born a flesh man; therefore, his ethnicity is based in the region of his birth.

When images are used to assert superiority and accentuate differences, this does not align with the heart of God.

The Church knows what Yeshua taught; however, we are not confronting the challenges necessary to become a diverse community of Disciples. *Evangelism* is our opportunity to invite people to share in the community of Disciples. There are numerous benefits within the community. However, *Evangelism* will prove difficult if the Church does not actively work towards becoming a community that shares things in common and cares for each other. Community membership was the only standard to receive care and assistance.

To be plain and clear, all images of God and Yeshua must be removed from every place of worship. These images have become a source of pride and divisiveness. In order to re-establish a focus on the Great Commission, to make Disciples of all nations, these images of divisiveness must be destroyed.

All nations must cause the community of Disciples to struggle with the internal and external conditions that will reveal that we are not like Yeshua. Prejudice and pride must be defeated, but in order to defeat them, the Church must first acknowledge that they exist within the Church. In Acts 6, it is clear that the Jews did not value the Greek widows the same as the Jewish widows. When the complaint was raised, the Apostles did not provide sensitivity training. They instructed them to identify seven mature disciples who could manage the food distribution. In order to refocus the Church, some people are going to need to be replaced. The community cannot continue to follow divisive people and expect to be effective in reaching all nations.

Doctrinal differences are the most prevalent issues that result in separation in the Church. This is the most difficult source of divisiveness because spiritual leaders do not work to dialogue about differences. This does not mean compromising the truth for community. It means we must invest in hearing different interpretations and allow the *Word* of God to resolve the issues. Every spiritual leader must seek to establish doctrine on the truth of the *Word* above and beyond the traditions of the Church.

The Evangelist must have answers for the issues in the community. Some people are intentionally avoiding the community of Disciples because they see us avoiding our issues instead of confronting them. The Evangelist cannot ignore or misrepresent the issues of the community. In order for *Evangelism* to be effective and successful, the evangelist must be prepared to share the love of God to secure a conscious commitment to learn, live, and share the teachings of Yeshua.

Evangelism fuels the Disciple-Making process by bringing in Disciple trainees and by being the vehicle for Disciples to be *Disciple Makers*. Without effective *Evangelism*, eventually the community of disciples will cease to exist.

The community will eventually die out. The importance of Disciple-Making is reflected in the life and passion of those who execute *Evangelism*. Every Disciple must be equipped to do *Evangelism*. This does not mean that every Disciple is an evangelist. An evangelist is a person who has been gifted and called to evangelize.

Their passion and focus are to claim the lost into the Kingdom of God. The Evangelist must be able and willing to prepare the community to be effective at *Evangelism* and to demonstrate effective *Evangelism* for the community of Disciples. The sole focus of an evangelist is to invite the world to a conscious commitment to become Disciples. The execution of *Evangelism* without a focus on making Disciples falls short of the Great Commission.

One way we can recognize the importance of Disciple-Making-focused *Evangelism* is by assessing the current state of the church. The traditional objective of *Evangelism* has been to lead the lost to confess faith and belief in God through Yeshua. The result is millions of people who claim to believe but are not willing to study, praise, or grow their relationship with God. The church does not reflect the Great Commission or the ministry model that Yeshua provided.

In Matthew 13, Yeshua teaches the *Parable of the Sower.* In verses 10-16, the disciples asked why He taught in parables.

They were concerned that some people would not understand the meaning of the parables. His response in verses 14-15:

> *"With them indeed is fulfilled the prophecy of Isaiah that says: 'You will indeed listen, but never understand, and you will indeed look, but never perceive. [15]For this people's heart has grown dull, and their ears are hard of hearing, and they have shut their eyes; so that they might not look with their eyes, and listen with their ears, and understand with their heart and turn— and I would heal them." Matthew 13:14-15NRSV*

This is what *Evangelism* has produced – believers who do not want to know or understand. *Evangelism* has generated messages that do not teach people how to be or make Disciples, but instead, produced individuals who are taught how to pursue blessings and invest in wealth and influence. The church has become so conditioned to respond to the flesh that any conversation about being and making Disciples falls on deaf ears. Verse 16 ends with Yeshua saying He would heal them. His desire is for the children of God to have a passion to live for God and represent God's standards and will in the world. This is no longer the focus of the church.

In verses 18-23, Yeshua explains the parable that He taught. The explanation is based on hearing the 'word' of the Kingdom. This is why Disciple Making should be the sole focus of the church. The Kingdom of God is founded on commitment and sacrifice, not material possessions, social influence, or political power.

- **The Path -** Those who hear the *Word* of the Kingdom but do not understand it. The evil one comes and snatches away what is in their heart. These individuals do not produce a commitment to grow or learn. This is what traditional *Evangelism* has produced when the people in the church do not care to understand. There is no passion to understand the teachings of Yeshua to grow in relationship with God. Just believing without commitment to being the Kingdom of God.

- **Rocky Ground** - Those who hear the *Word* of the Kingdom and receive it with joy, but they do not develop roots. They fail to establish a committed relationship; consequently, when trouble or persecution arises on account of the *Word*, they immediately fall away. It is important to note that the church is fostering rocky ground when the people within it do not even want to hear a *Word* about being the

Kingdom of God. When a commitment to Disciple Making is foreign to the church, we have become rocky ground. This is what traditional *Evangelism* produces: people who believe but lack commitment to growth and strength so they can withstand trouble and persecution.

- **Among Thorns** - Those who heard the *Word* of the Kingdom, but the cares of the world and the lure of wealth have choked the *Word* out. This is what the church produces when messages focus on life issues and the pursuit of wealth. The *Word* of the Kingdom is meant to focus Disciples on being and making Disciples. Ministers are not intended to be 'life coaches.' The standards and objectives of the Kingdom are what the church is to pursue.
- **Good Soil** - Those who hear the *Word* of the Kingdom and understand it. Their understanding leads them to produce a hundred, sixty, and thirty times. This soil represents people. The church is meant to

produce Disciples who are good soil. They are eager to understand and cultivate. The intention of this teaching is to inform Disciples that they need to demonstrate that they are Good Soil.

Everyone hears the 'word' and has some form of a positive response to it. However, the objective is to be Good Soil that cultivates more Disciples. Every other condition is temporary and does not satisfy the objective of the 'word' of the Kingdom. The church must share the 'word' of the Kingdom to produce Good Soil. Good soil is not a church that you give money to. Good soil is the evidence of a committed Disciple. Good soil is how believers evaluate themselves and each other. The people in the church should be asking themselves and each other, "What kind of ground am I?" Only when Disciples are reproducing Disciples can we call ourselves Good Soil. Then the focus becomes the rate of our reproduction.

How did Yeshua speak so clearly, yet the church has moved so far from His instructions? We have allowed people to represent God who have had motives that were not from the Kingdom. We have allowed the evil one to infiltrate the pulpit. We have allowed the evil one to come with a 'word' that satisfies us more than God. We have driven out any focus on being a committed Disciple by saying we do not have time, or this teaching is not practical. How can the words of Yeshua not be practical to His church?

Evangelism that lacks a clear understanding of its objective does not assist the church or advance the Kingdom of God. Ultimately, it damages the mission and fosters a church that fails to represent the example or teachings of Yeshua. This is why we must do the hard work to reform the church and transform *Evangelism* to have a Disciple Making focus.

Any *Evangelism* effort that does not seek to produce a Disciple Making commitment is counterproductive and not seeking to fulfill the teachings of Yeshua.

Invitation to Disciple Making

Invitation to Discipleship (disciple-making) is a phrase used in some worship flows. Traditionally, this is the time in the worship service when the 'doors of the church are opened.' I remember being a little child dreading this part of the worship service because it always seemed to be the part that took the longest. In some traditional settings, this is when salvation and/or church membership are offered after the sermon.

Often, I remember the altar workers helping individuals repent of their sins and call on the name of the Lord to be saved, but afterward, there was no talk of commitment.

Usually, the only thing the Church Mother would mention after people 'got saved' was all the things they couldn't do, or else they would go to hell. The Church had the right intention but the wrong information and language. *Evangelism* has been used to bring people to the worship service, and the invitation has been used to offer salvation and church membership. We must talk about the two.

In Matthew 7:24–27, at the end of the *Sermon on the Mount*, Yeshua offers an invitation to Disciple Making. His invitation should have established the standard for how people are invited to become Disciples. There is nothing wrong with offering salvation or church membership, but the key commitment is to first becoming a Disciple. If we miss or leave out this commitment, the church ends up with saved people who have no commitment to advance the teachings of Yeshua or the Kingdom of God. The Church ends up having services without impact because the members are not focused on the mission of salvation – to make Disciples of all nations.

The church must know and accept that some people do not understand what it means to be saved; therefore, we must be willing to allow them to learn so that they understand the power of the grace that God is offering in salvation.

The focus of *Evangelism* must be to invite people to become Disciples. This commitment is to learn, live, and share the teachings of Yeshua.

At the end of the Sermon on the Mount (Matthew 5 – 7), Yeshua uses the example of two people who have built houses. They are built on the same and experience the same conditions. There is only one difference between the two houses. The difference between the two houses is their foundations – one is built on *Sand* and the other is built on *Rock*.
He clearly states in Matthew 7 verses 24 and 26 that the *Rock* and *Sand* are based on a decision:

> *"Everyone then who hears these words of mine and acts on them" is like a person who built on rock. "Everyone then who hears these words of mine and does not act on them" is like a person who built on sand. The house built on rock withstood the storm, but the house built on sand fell in the storm. Matthew 7:24 & 26 NRSV*

The invitation that Yeshua offered was to learn, live, and share His teachings. Those who make this commitment will be built on *Rock,* and those who do not will be built on *Sand.*

Committing to be a Disciple does not mean that we are exempt from storms. It means that we endure them differently because we allow the teachings of Yeshua to navigate our life.

This invitation to Disciple Making was not made in the synagogue. *Evangelism* must conclude with an invitation to become a *Disciple Maker.* We are inviting people to make a commitment to learn, live, and share the teachings of Yeshua. They must know this is a lifelong commitment. They do not have to know what Yeshua taught to make a commitment to learn.

The commission is to make Disciples. This can happen during a worship experience, but it is more effective to seek this commitment before we invite people to worship. The purpose of corporate worship is for God's children to celebrate God. Disciples are made in our daily lives as we interact with the world. As we share Yeshua with people and live His principles and standards, we should be planning and preparing to ask if the person wants to become a Disciple of Yeshua. Then, we invite them into a community that is focused on learning, living, and sharing the teachings of Yeshua.

We have allowed the focus of the church to be clouded to the point that some people do not see the value or need to be part of a community of Disciples. When making Disciples is the focus of the community, everyone will see the value and need to be within a community.

Some may be concerned that this approach may not lead some people to accept Yeshua as Lord and Savior. This is correct. Some people may start learning and decide this is not what they want. The traditional model of *Evangelism* sought to secure a confession of salvation and maybe get the person to join the church. But less than ten percent of church members participate in prayer or bible study regularly, while one hundred percent of the church is saved. How does this reality honor the Great Commission?

> *"Because of this many of his Disciples turned back and no longer went about with him."*
> John 6:66 NRSV

The setting is that Yeshua instructed them to eat His flesh and drink His blood. The disciples concluded that this teaching was hard, maybe because they took Him literally. Therefore, many disciples stopped following Him.

The disciples turned back, and some in the crowd stopped following Him. Disciples left Him because of what He taught.

They knew that as disciples, they had made a commitment to learn, live, and share His teachings. Whenever a disciple arrived at a point when they could not or would not live by a teaching, they understood that they were no longer a disciple. They did not fake their commitment because being a disciple was very important to them. If they were not going to follow a teaching, they would find another teacher that they were willing to follow.

Why has "no" become an unacceptable response in the church? Yeshua did not force people to maintain their initial commitment, so why should we? In the Bible, people responded, "no." This invitation must allow a person to say, "no." *Evangelism* is only looking to the people who respond, "yes," with the willingness to pursue the teachings of Yeshua wholeheartedly. "Maybe" means "no" for right now. *Evangelism* cannot populate the community of Disciples with people who are not fully committed. Just as Ananias and Sapphira died and Simon was instructed to repent, we must protect the integrity and the intent of the community by populating it with sincerely committed people.

This does not mean that Disciples will be perfect, but it does mean that we will value correction. We will learn from testimonies and seek to grow from every situation.

Those who respond, "yes" to the invitation will live to bear witness that their life is built on *Rock* by living the teachings of Yeshua. If someone comes to the point where they cannot or will not adhere to a teaching, there is no need to debate the teaching. This means they no longer want to be a Disciple. This happened to Yeshua, so we must prepare for this to happen to us.

The objective of *Evangelism* is to offer a commitment to learn, live, and share the teachings of Yeshua. One of these teachings is to believe in Yeshua to be reconnected and committed to the Father through grace. Then we are willing to learn and grow. This process of development requires a willingness to be held accountable for our progress in learning, living, and sharing.

Everyone who seeks to evangelize must be a committed Disciple. We cannot invite people to a commitment that we have not made. The failure of *Evangelism* begins in the reality that the church is not producing Disciples. The question at this point is,

"Are you a committed Disciple? Or are you simply a saved person?" Have you made a conscious commitment to learn, live, and share the teachings of Yeshua?

You should not seek to evangelize until you have confirmed your commitment to be a Disciple. Then you can simply ask people to follow you. *Evangelism* becomes easy when we are inviting people to a journey that we are on. This requires accepting "no" as a response.

If a person does not want to become a committed Disciple of Yeshua, don't offer them a substitute. Don't offer them salvation if they are not willing to pursue God with their life. Don't invite them to church if they are not willing to commit to learning and growing. The church is for believers. The church is for those who are at least willing to learn what it means to be a Disciple. The church is not for entertainment. It is for Disciples to learn and worship. Our unwillingness to make Disciples has turned the church into everything but Disciple training and accountability.

Relationship Evangelism

One of the methods of *Evangelism* being used and written about is *Relationship Evangelism*. This is basically where the evangelist seeks to develop a relationship with the target for Disciple Making. Then, as a component of the relationship, the target is able to observe the life of a Disciple.

The plan is based on the example and the strength of the relationship. The target ultimately desires to make a commitment to become a *Disciple Maker* and walks this journey with their Disciple Making mentor.

This method requires the *Disciple Makers* to understand that they must have Disciple Making as the focus and core of the relationship. Failures, negative impacts, or issues in the relationship can impact the target's willingness to commit to following Yeshua. Also, the desire to maintain good standing with one another in the relationship can impact the instruction and rebuke that will need to be provided to foster growth.

I actually encountered this relationship with a friend I was Discipling relationally last year. We would meet regularly, talk about the principles of the *Word*, and talk about its application to life. She would generally let me know where she 'fell short' that week and I typically would encourage her. I always felt a little uneasy when trying to push her to grow further in the teachings of Yeshua because I was worried about trying to keep her around as a friend instead of keeping Disciple Making as the focus of our relationship.

This is why the *Relationship Evangelism* method can become clouded because of the relationship. Relationships of every kind have issues. There are no perfect relationships, but there are relationships that are so significant to us that we are willing to work to maintain them. How long does it take to develop a relationship that is worth working through difficulties and issues? To address the issues of *Relationship Evangelism*, the Church included "*Small Groups*".

Small Groups are effective because the group's dynamics assist to expand the relationship dynamics from one-on-one to the group impacting the target. *Small Groups* also offer the opportunity for the target to be exposed to the example and teachings of Yeshua in the group. If the objective of the group is something other than Disciple Making, it may become difficult to introduce Disciple Making into the group.

The shortcoming of *Small Groups* is when the group's focus is not Disciple Making. For example, a Small Group that is focused on golf, is a group that is able to attract people who are interested in golf. The objective is to pray before they play and through the prayer, the group is exposed to Yeshua and some principles of His teachings. By observing the core team members' interactions and life's examples, the other members of the group will become interested in pursuing Disciple Making. There is nothing wrong with this approach, but some group members may feel exploited or misled when the group shifts to becoming a Disciple. The target has invested time and become comfortable with their golf group to find out that they were just looking to make Disciples.

I am not saying that this method is not effective. I am saying that the core group members must be mature and able to be aware of the appropriate time to introduce a commitment to Disciple Making. As with *Relationship Evangelism* in general, missing the appropriate time or issues in the group or relationship will impact the ability to advance to a Disciple Making commitment.

Relationship Evangelism of any form, Small Group, or otherwise, limits the potential Disciples who can be targeted. People cannot maintain 20-30 relationships simultaneously; this is not productive or healthy.

Small Groups are usually limited to 15 or fewer people so that the group can effectively be managed. These restrictions can lead to *Homogeneous Evangelism*.

Homogeneous Evangelism - The targets become people who are just like us. Most people are not seeking to be uncomfortable in their relationships, so we do not seek to interact with people who are substantially different from us. Generally, people seek commonality in relationships, such as those who live in the same area, have children that go to the same school, or have common interests, such as golf or sewing. This may be one of the reasons that the Church is not diverse. This may be how the Church consciously or unconsciously avoided making Disciples of all nations.

There can be difficult and awkward times when the target is the minority in the community of Disciples. There is a feeling that they must comply with the socio-economic standards, language, and prevailing philosophies of the majority. This can very easily cause the target to become disingenuous in an attempt to fit in. The target can also start to feel like a mission project because they do not fit in.

In *Relationship Evangelism*, the Church must be ready and willing to engage in difficult topics and issues in order to pursue the diversity that Yeshua intended. There must be intentional opportunities to allow minorities in the community to voice their feelings and thoughts, especially those that may challenge the opinions and preferences of the majority.

Homogeneous Evangelism may not have been the objective of *Relationship Evangelism*, but it is easy to recognize. Simply analyze the composition of your community. If the overwhelming majority of members are in multiple homogeneous categories, then somehow discipling all nations and people has been missed. This does not mean that *Relationship Evangelism* is ineffective and should be avoided. To the contrary, when the community recognizes that they have cultivated a homogeneous community based on any category, this is a call to action. The community must challenge itself to do two things:

Use their commonality against themselves so that they are challenged to grow. For example, a community of Disciples that is overwhelmingly from the same economic condition can intentionally use their economic status to seek out people who are not like them. In order to reverse the homogeneous condition, the community must be honest with the diverse target and acknowledge this condition, expressing their desire to reverse it. A community of lower-income people may seek to evangelize in communities with different income levels and honestly inform them that they are seeking to benefit from diversity, extending an invitation to join them. I strongly believe that Yeshua wants His Disciples to face the challenges of diversity because this requires maturity and sincerity. It is necessary for the community to understand and be willing to state the need and the benefits that come with diversity. This is required for change and growth in the community because they will intentionally seek to develop beyond their homogeneous categories.

- Identify the prevailing commonality categories and challenge the community to intentionally seek to diversify. The commonalities must also be used to inform the community of their comfort zones and why these areas have become comfort zones. Are there fears or discomforts that the community has unconsciously allowed to enter? Is there some form of identity issue or philosophy that is shared in the community that has not been addressed? The homogeneous condition is evident of something that is shared within the community. The community must invest in identifying what those things are so that they can diversify and benefit from the diversity.

Relationship Evangelism offers some great opportunities for disciple making and community growth if leadership is willing to honestly evaluate its success. By evaluating the areas where *Evangelism* is successful, the community can identify opportunities for growth. There are powerful lessons to learn from success. Many times, leadership focuses on correcting failures to achieve success. I have learned that it is better to focus on the areas of success to provide growth opportunities for the community while simultaneously teaching about the power and benefits of diversity.

Relationship Evangelism can be a powerful method to make Disciples, but we must be mindful of homogeneous results. While we seek to expand the community of Disciples, we must also challenge the community to appreciate and embrace the diversity of God's creation.

Confrontational Evangelism

Confrontational Evangelism is when a Disciple directly confronts a non-believer to invite them to believe in Yeshua as their personal Lord and Savior, and to commit to following His teachings as their intentional lifestyle.

As with any method of *Evangelism*, there are strengths and weaknesses to this approach. The prevailing strength is that the intention of the interaction is clear and unavoidable. This method leaves no room for ambiguity. The Disciple gets straight to the point of sharing the Gospel with the world.

> "Will you surrender your life to the lordship of Yeshua and will you give your life to learn, live, and share His teachings? Yes or No?" Remember that even in *Relational Evangelism*, the Disciple must find the time and way to ask a person the same question.

In *Confrontational Evangelism*, the evangelist starts with the question and then interacts with the person to help them understand how to arrive at an answer.

The failure of *Confrontational Evangelism* is that a quick response may not yield a lasting impact. For this method to be effective, the evangelist will have to maintain daily contact with the new Disciple in order to transition them into the community. People have learned to say yes or no and move on, knowing that the evangelist is only looking for a response, not a relationship. People have also learned to say yes out of compulsion in order to not offend or reject the *Disciple Maker*.

I remember years ago being at a conference and witnessing a *Confrontational Evangelism* attempt on a lady in front of other people. I could see the pressure, attention, and focus all being put on this lady, who I truly believe loved God but felt the only way she could get out of the confrontation with the *Disciple Maker* was to give them what they wanted – a yes! Therefore, gaining a false confession just so the *Disciple Maker* is pleased, and the lady can get out of the 'hot seat' is just as damaging and will not last.

Effective *Evangelism* requires both confrontation and relationship. The only difference between Relational and *Confrontational Evangelism* is the flow of the interaction. *Confrontational Evangelism* has been the historical method of *Evangelism*. It requires the evangelist to stay focused on their mission and objective, which is to cultivate new Disciples.

However, the evangelist cannot become so focused on the question or desired outcome that they lose the opportunity to invite the person to become a *Disciple*

Making Disciple. Once the person declares their faith and commitment to Yeshua as their personal Lord and Savior, it is imperative that the new Disciple joins the community of Disciples. Most Confrontational Evangelists win the battle but lose the war. A confession without a commitment to be discipled is not fulfilling the commission of Yeshua. This is another reason why there are so many people that are "saved" but not committed to being Disciples.

Whether the evangelist uses *Confrontational* or Relational *Evangelism,* the strengths of both methods must be employed. The hybrid of these two methods is *Evangelism.* The question of belief and commitment must be presented at some point, whether in the beginning or after a relationship is established. A relationship is necessary for the new Disciple to get acclimated into the community.

Evangelists have become so focused on pitting these methods against each other to the point that neither method is totally effective. The evangelist must be discerning because no method is going to fit every person. The evangelist must be prepared to ask 'The

Questions' and initiate relationships. The effectiveness of *Evangelism* is not in the method that is employed. It is in the evangelist being able to determine the best approach for the person they are interacting with. Some people will respond best to a direct question while others will respond to a relational invitation to get to know some disciples before being asked the question.

This flexibility is required to be an effective evangelist. Learn to listen to the person so that you will know how to evangelize them. People will share their experiences, even their understanding of Yeshua and the church if asked. The more information the evangelist is willing to gather, the more effective they can be.

The objective is to make Disciples, not to receive confessions of belief. The confrontation is a necessary part of *Evangelism*, but it is not the objective. Making Disciples begins with a confession and commitment. The evangelist must secure both before the person is transitioned to the community.

Remember, *Successful Evangelism* is assisting the person to confess Yeshua as Lord and commit to learn, live, and share His teachings. This is the point when the new Disciple is transitioned into the community of Disciples. The evangelist is not merely inviting people to church; they are inviting them into a relationship with Yeshua through the church.

Miracles as a Method of Evangelism

It is impossible to overlook the correlation between miracles and attracting people in the New Testament. Yeshua used miracles to teach, demonstrate who sent Him, and draw crowds. While other methods of *Evangelism* have their merits, we cannot ignore the effectiveness of miracles in the ministry of Yeshua and the disciples who followed Him. Take some time to study how Yeshua used miracles as a tool to teach and attract. We will focus on one example in Acts 8:4-8. Philip, one of the seven selected to manage the food distribution to the widows, arrived in a city called Samaria when the disciples disbursed because of the great persecution Saul started.

When Philip arrived in this foreign city, he did not know anyone and was unfamiliar with their customs and beliefs. All he knew was what he had been taught and seen. While the disciples were fleeing Jerusalem to save their natural lives, they fled with intention and purpose. They understood that their purpose was to impact the world with the message of Yeshua the Christ (The Gospel), so Philip entered this foreign town with the intention of impacting them with the power of the Holy Spirit and the message of Yeshua. Verse 6 references "hearing and seeing," which must be encompassed for effective *Evangelism*. People must hear the clear message of Yeshua and see evidence of God through the Holy Spirit. This is what makes miracles, signs, and wonders the gold standard of *Evangelism*.

I know what you are thinking. How do we get miracle-working power? The New Testament does not give us a checklist for how to receive power, but it does tell us what the disciples did to prepare for the power of the Holy Spirit. Before we discuss receiving the power of the Holy Spirit, it is important to note that the disciples did not focus on the ability to execute miracles. They just trusted the Holy Spirit. For example, in Acts 9, Ananias is sent to restore Saul's sight. He never asked how he was to accomplish this. He was so confident that the miracle would happen that he was focused on what would happen after the miracle was completed. Power in the Kingdom is focused on availability, not ability.

We must know that God does not fail; therefore, anything that we do to expand the Kingdom will be accompanied by the power and will of God. Yeshua nor the disciples used spiritual power for their own needs or situations. Even the healing of Peter's mother-in-law was preparing Peter to respond to his *Calling* (Luke 4:38).

> *After leaving the synagogue he entered Simon's house. Now Simon's mother-in-law was suffering from a high fever, and they asked him about her. Luke 4:38 NRSV*

What do we know about being empowered with the Holy Spirit?

- Acts 1:8 – As Yeshua was preparing to ascend, he instructed the disciples that they would receive power when the Holy Spirit came upon them to be witnesses for Him.

> *"But you will receive power when the Holy Spirit has come upon you; and you will be my witnesses in Jerusalem, in all Judea and Samaria, and to the ends of the earth." Acts 1:8 NRSV*

There are two lessons in this verse:

- We must be Disciples. This means that we are committed to learning, living, and sharing what Yeshua taught. The presence of the Holy Spirit came upon 120 disciples in the Upper Room. These disciples had been with Yeshua and received His teachings. They were not new disciples. They were committed, trained, and prepared. We cannot seek to receive the power of the Holy Spirit until we have demonstrated an unwavering commitment to learning, living, and sharing His teachings.

- We must be willing to be witnesses. This is not an occasional *Evangelism* activity. Being a witness is a lifetime commitment to represent God through Yeshua by the Holy Spirit everywhere and at all times. There is no on-and-off switch for witnessing. The lifetime commitment of a Disciple is to witness for Yeshua anywhere and anytime. We must make conscious life changes to be a witness continually.

- Acts 2:1 (King James Version) – the KJV is the only version that has this language and I think this language is very important; "with one accord". "When the day of Pentecost was fully come, they were all with one accord in one place."
    - The disciples spent ten days in the same place. To achieve being on one accord, some issues had to be addressed. Peter had denied Yeshua,

Thomas had doubted, Judas was dead, and Matthias had been selected in his place. The Holy Spirit did not enter people who were in chaos and confusion. The Holy Spirit entered people who were in agreement and eager to face whatever the Gospel would cost them.

- Many spiritual communities (churches) are not on one accord, and we are not willing to do the hard work to get there, but we expect God to send the Holy Spirit so that we can execute miracles. Being a *Disciple Making* community means we work to trust each other and depend on each other. This does not happen in an empowerment session. It happens with the hard work of developing relationships and giving room for our diversity.
- One accord does not mean that we will function the same. It means that we will respect how God desires to work with each

of us. All of the apostles were different, but they respected the position Peter was given and they followed him. Peter allowed each apostle to be who they were called to be as long as they did not stray from the teachings of Yeshua.

- The Holy Spirit presence/power is not intended to be an individual experience. It is intended to be a community experience. We tend to be and think selfishly; "I want the Holy Spirit." Our mindset should be, "the community needs the Holy Spirit." We should be hungry for those who are committed and prepared to receive the power of the Holy Spirit even if that is not you or me.

The Holy Spirit came to give them the power to be witnesses. The evidence of the event was that they witnessed to the people that were present. The Holy Spirit handled the language barrier. They just had to be hungry to share Yeshua with the people. At times we get the focus confused by desiring the gift of tongue instead of desiring the ability to share the Gospel message with all nations. I pray that you can see the difference. The power of the Holy Spirit is to empower Disciples to be witnesses to all nations. Our desire cannot simply be to prove that we have the power of the Holy Spirit by speaking in an unknown language or performing some other miracle, sign, or wonder.

- There is no information in scripture that teaches us that Yeshua or any of the disciples prayed to know what miracles to present. As with Philip, they addressed the issues in front of them not based on the resources they had, but by the power of the Holy Spirit. The action that
makes miracles, signs, and wonders so powerful is that they are beyond our ability and resources.

- Miracles as a method of *Evangelism* accomplishes two objectives just by the evidence of the miracle:
    - People receive evidence that God is real.
    - People will know that God cares about them because the miracle addressed their need or the person who received the miracle's need.

Philip could move very quickly to an invitation to Disciple Making because the people not only heard, but they also saw God through Yeshua. *Evangelism* invests a lot of time in convincing people that God is real and cares for them, when our faith in the power of the Holy Spirit can impact people in profound ways.

Disciples must grow to trust in the Lord. Invest in ingesting.

> *"Trust in the Lord with all your heart, and do not rely on your own insight. In all your ways acknowledge Him, and He will make straight your paths." Proverbs 3:5-6 NRSV*

Sign - conveys information about how God feels about a situation or condition. A Sign can also confirm God's intention or direction. Signs are information about God.

Wonder - an action that causes amazement, excitement or surprise.

Miracle - alters, reverses, or eliminates a physical condition or situation by spiritual power.

Your Role in Evangelism

I hope it is crystal clear that the first and most important decision is that you confess Yeshua as your Savior and commit to surrendering to Him as your Lord. This is not simply a confession.

You must seek God to plant yourself in a Disciple Making focused community (church) so that you can develop into a mature Disciple who is prepared to represent Yeshua to the world in the power of the Holy Spirit.

Learn from the many examples of how Yeshua impacted people where they were. He used every situation to impact people to become Disciples. He challenged the religious establishment because they thought they did not need Him. He encouraged the faith of a centurion who did not think he was worthy to have Yeshua come to his home. He executed miracles when the religious establishment said it was unlawful. This is why it is so important to grow and be consumed in the Holy Spirit.

There is an exact roadmap for *Evangelism*. *Evangelism* must function in the flow of life. Every situation is an opportunity to evangelize if you are prepared and willing. We must stop treating *Evangelism* as a special function or event.

Evangelism is a gift from the Holy Spirit, but it is also a commission on the life of every Disciple. We are inviting the world to confess and commit. You cannot invite people to a relationship that you are not pursuing.

It all becomes easier when you are inviting people into the journey that you are pursuing.

In Luke 10:2, Yeshua informed the disciples that the harvest is plentiful, but the laborers are few.

> *He said to them, "The harvest is plentiful, but the laborers are few; therefore, ask the Lord of the harvest to send out laborers into his harvest. Luke 10:2 NRSV*

The harvest that you must seek exists in two very different fields.

- People are lost in the church, so you must be willing to share with church members that there is more to a relationship with God through Yeshua than attending worship and praying occasionally. As Disciples of Yeshua, we have been commissioned to become *Disciple Makers.*

- People are lost in the world, so you must prepare every day to be *led* and commanded by the Holy Spirit to see every encounter and situation as an opportunity to share Yeshua as the solution.

The harvest is not just in the lost world; it also includes the lost and misinformed church. Two very different approaches are needed to reap these harvests. In the church, you will need to share information and confront traditions that may have caused the church to veer off track. The church is not going to embrace or welcome this invasion of their comfort zone.

The world is very skeptical and often convinced that faith and commitment to Yeshua are signs of weakness. Many times, we end up defending our faith instead of sharing it. There is no need to defend our faith. Just as the world has the right to refuse Yeshua, we have the right to believe and follow. You will need to learn to differentiate between defending your faith and sharing

Yeshua so that others can confess and commit. The simple way to identify when you are defending and not presenting is if you invest most, if not all, of your conversation on why you believe.

Asking people if they believe and are committed can be very uncomfortable. We must remember that we are sharing life with them. Actually, we are sharing 'life more abundantly.' It is fine if they refuse. That is their right. "No," has to be an acceptable response because it is best for them to be honest.

Yeshua saves, not us.

> "No one can serve two masters, for a slave will either hate the one and love the other or be devoted
> to the one and despise the other. You cannot serve God and wealth. Matthew 6:24 NRSV

> "No slave can serve two masters, for a slave will either hate the one and love the other or be devoted to the one and despise the other. You cannot serve God and wealth" Luke 16:13 NRSV

Matthew 6:24 and Luke 16:13 state that we cannot love two masters. We will hate one and love the other. Everyone must decide which master they will love. Denying God, Yeshua, or the Holy Spirit means that we do not want to invest our faith in the Creator of the universe or the Savior of humankind. In order to function effectively, you must be prepared and okay with the church and the world rejecting the truth. Both rejected Yeshua, but He sought to embrace those that would believe and commit.

While confessing and committing are optional for the world and the church, it is not optional for Disciples to be *Disciple Makers*.

Your confession and commitment to Yeshua offer you the gracious opportunity to share the grace of God with everyone you meet so they can receive the Kingdom of God as you have. You must clearly understand what it means to be a Disciple so that as you invest in Disciple Making, you will understand the growth process.

It is important to have a community that is in agreement with the process and method of making Disciples so that you can be encouraged and supported as you seek to grow as a Disciple and invest in making Disciples. There are a lot of challenges on this journey. You must have someone who is willing to invest in you so that you do not lose heart.

NOTES

Adult Disciple Development
(Spiritual Age is 35 – 69 years)

"They are ready to carry the full responsibility of nurturing others through their life example and knowledge."

The *Adult Disciple* is a leader. They have been spiritually developed and are now a committed *Disciple Maker*. They lead a disciplined lifestyle with the Kingdom of God as their sole priority. They are confident in their development and preparedness to represent Yeshua to the world. While the *Adult Disciple* is responsible for the development and protection of the disciple-making community, they also need encouragement and guidance from *Senior Disciples*.

They must remain humble and open to the anointing and experience of *Senior Disciples* for their continued development. There must be a mutual respect among the *Adult Disciples*. They must demonstrate a willingness to be *Disciple*

Makers and protect the community's integrity at all costs without compromise.

Adult Disciples must interact with each other for encouragement and direction.

> *The Adult Disciples learn from*
> *each other through sharing of*
> *experiences and revelation.*

MINISTRY LEVEL

The *Adult Disciples* are the teachers, proclaimers of the Word, and developers of disciples. They carry out the work of ministry, training and supervising the disciple-making community. There is no separate group called ministers; the ministers in the community are the Spiritually Mature. The level of ministry is not determined by *Calling* but by maturity. All *Adult Disciples* should be willing to teach others and proclaim the *Word* of God to the community of disciples and the world. Leaders in the community must be the result of spiritual growth and maturity. Those who lead the community must be the product of their development within the community. These leaders include pastors, bishops, apostles, prophets, teachers, evangelists, and elders. They are the leaders of the community of disciples.

Outline

Understanding and Executing Spiritual Warfare

The Apostle Paul informs us that our fight is not against people but against the rulers, against the authorities, against the cosmic powers of this present darkness, against the spiritual forces of evil in the heavenly places.

> *"For our struggle is not against blood and flesh but against the rulers, against the authorities, against the cosmic powers of this present darkness, against the spiritual forces of evil in the heavenly places."* Ephesians 6:12
> NRSV

Paul instructs the disciples to put on the whole (complete) armor of God (Ephesians 6:10-20). Disciples who engage in spiritual warfare do not fight for themselves or by themselves. Spiritual warfare is executed for the community of disciples by the community of disciples. Unity and oneness are the foundational tools for successful spiritual warfare. Spiritual Warfare is not optional.

Every disciple must mature to be a soldier fighting for the Kingdom of God.

The armor is seven-character attributes that mature disciples must demonstrate to fight in spiritual warfare:

- Truth – Disciples must live it and tell it. Living the truth means living the teachings of Yeshua. Telling the truth means conveying the *Word* and will of God. Disciples are to be honorable and not lie, but here Paul is preparing disciples to fight spiritual battles.

The truth is in Yeshua; therefore, the *Word* of God and Yeshua's teachings must be the truth that we fight with spiritually.

- Righteousness – These characteristics are in a specific order because we cannot be righteous without first adhering to the truth. Being righteous means adhering to the *Word* and will of God. Disciples cannot have faults or be guilty of accusations. This does not mean we cannot make mistakes or sin. It means that we acknowledge our faults and sins. We repent (request to be changed) of them and strive to please God with our lives.
- Proclaim the Gospel of peace – Disciples are always witnesses of the reality of Yeshua the Messiah everywhere and at all times. Disciples cannot be silent.

We must be willing to speak the *Word* and will of God whenever the Holy Spirit instructs us to. To fight in this spiritual war, we must proclaim the word.

- Faith – This is not referring to faith for salvation. The Ephesians are already saved. This is faith to know that these spiritual enemies are defeated, and we have the power with Yeshua to defend and defeat every attack.

- Salvation – Just like faith, this is not telling the Ephesians to be saved. Paul is writing to disciples who are already saved. He wants them to be reassured in their salvation. One of the weapons of the enemy is self-doubt. Spiritual forces of evil work hard to cause disciples to doubt who we are and what we can accomplish for the Kingdom.

- Spirit – This is a two-fold weapon. It is defensive and offensive. The Spirit defends disciples through direction and correction. The Spirit keeps disciples in God's will and empowers us to do God's will effectively. The Spirit is offensive in two ways:

- First, the Spirit attacks the enemy. Disciples can challenge the attacks of the enemy.

  Disciples must learn to be proactive. Don't wait for an attack. We know there are spiritual forces of evil; therefore, we can attack them at every chance.

- Second, the Spirit is offensive in that we will offend sin and sinners. Flowing in this spiritual armor will offend everyone who is not willing to surrender to the *Word* and will of God. This is why disciples must function from a posture of love and humility. We cannot seek to avoid offending sin. We must proclaim

God's truth in love and humility. Spiritual forces of evil want to stop us from using our armor by causing us to doubt the power of the armor we possess.

- Prayer – Paul defines prayer as a weapon against the enemy when it is used in three ways:
- Pray in the Spirit all the time – this means our prayers are *led* by the Spirit. Disciples cannot just pray for what we need, want, and think. We must be yielded to the Spirit to the point that the Spirit governs what we pray.
- Pray for each other – disciples are to pray for our fellow disciples regularly. We are to join in battle with each other so that everyone has victory over the enemy. This is the power of intercession. The intercessor joins in spiritual warfare with other disciples. Disciples must be *led* by the Spirit to know when we must fight with and for others.

- Paul requests for the Ephesians to pray for him. This means every disciple must be praying for spiritual leaders, especially the leaders they are connected to.

In Ephesians 4:11-12, Paul taught that specific spiritual leaders have been positioned to equip the disciples for the work of ministry.

> *He himself granted that some are apostles, prophets, evangelists, pastors and teachers to equip the saints for the work of ministry, for building up the body of Christ." Ephesians 4:11-12* NRSV

Disciples must pray for the protection and strengthening of these ministry *Gifts* in the Kingdom.

Praying for our spiritual leaders means praying for these ministry *Gifts* to be protected and present in our disciple community: Apostles, Prophets, Evangelists, Pastors, and Teachers.

Now that we understand the characteristics we must live by, let's understand Spiritual Warfare.

What is Spiritual Warfare?

There are two perspectives to understanding Spiritual Warfare:

- **Fighting against spiritual forces of evil** – This perspective is reactive. We fight after the enemy has attacked. This is necessary but not always effective. Disciples can be wounded, distracted, and defeated because the community of disciples only respond to an attack.

- **Fighting for the Kingdom of God** – A better approach to Spiritual Warfare is to understand it as fighting for the Kingdom of God. Every disciple must take their shift on the wall to protect the community and watch for where the enemy will attempt an attack. This is proactive.

Every disciple must be willing to function in coordination with their disciple community to watch and fight to protect their community and every disciple in the community.

When we engage in Spiritual Warfare, these components must be present:

- **Focused** – We cannot fight spiritual forces of evil while multitasking or with distractions in our environment. Spiritual Warfare demands us to be focused on the task at hand. The enemy wants to steal, kill, and destroy. To fight against these forces means we must have time to be focused on defending disciples and defeating every attack.
- **Selfless** – We should not engage in Spiritual Warfare alone or just for ourselves. Spiritual

Warfare is best executed in numbers, in agreement. The instructions for warfare must be specific and strategic. We cannot simply ask disciples to pray. We must invest in multifaceted attacks against
spiritual forces of evil. Squadrons of disciples must be intentionally positioned to attack the enemy from different positions at the same time. If every disciple is attacking for themselves, we lose the power of unity and agreement. We must be selfless and focused.

- **Declaration of War** – To engage in a legitimate war, there must be a declaration of war first. The declaration defines what we are fighting for and against. This allows us to know who the enemy is and when victory has been achieved. The declaration allows every disciple to know their task in the war. Spiritual leaders must define the strategy and assignments in the spiritual war. Disciples must have the boldness to tell the enemy we are going to fight and win. The enemy must know we are not going to allow the spiritual forces of evil to impact or control the life or peace of Yeshua's disciples. Let's fight under a proclaimed declaration of war.

- **Willing to Engage** – Some disciples are not prepared to engage the enemy. Some disciples need to mature before they engage in Spiritual Warfare. Those who are mature must remain ready to engage in warfare. We must be on watch for demons and attacks. We have been so distracted that the enemy has positioned spirits in the community of disciples. We must engage to cleanse the community first. This is not about people or personalities.

  We battle against spiritual forces of evil. Engagement may be required at any time; therefore, disciples must be ready to receive orders to engage at any time. These orders can come from the Spirit, spiritual leaders, or another disciple (in this order).

- **Civilian Casualties** – We cannot engage in warfare without being prepared for civilian casualties. The enemy doesn't just attack the soldiers who have enlisted in the war. The enemy will attack civilians who are attached to the soldiers. The enemy understands we have access to victory; consequently, we will be distracted by attacks on the civilians we care about. Do not think the enemy is going to fight fairly or that weaknesses within us will not be exploited. It is important to minister to our family first and to cover them in God's words and prayer regularly. I witnessed Barbara Fite (my dear wife) release a 'word' that stuck with me: assign a scripture to each family member and pray for them from this assigned scripture covering. As we engage in attacking the enemy, we must be reassured that God will protect the civilians attached to us.

There will be times when there will be civilian casualties. Let's not blame God for the attack of the enemy. This is a war. It is sad but true; there will be casualties.

- **Defend the Kingdom and Its Citizens** – Spiritual Warfare includes healing, restoration, casting out demons, reclaiming authority from the enemy, etc. Spiritual Warfare is not only engaged in through prayer. Soldiers must engage the enemy on all fronts. When a demon is identified, we must be prepared to engage.
- **Be Offensive, Not Just Defensive** – Mature disciples must be coordinated and intentional. We must respond to the attacks of the enemy but also watch for opportunities to defeat attacks before they are executed and to impact the spiritual forces of evil to push them back.

NOTES

Senior Disciple Development
(Spiritual Age is 70 – 80 years)

"The Senior Disciple is to be honored through adherence to their teaching and imitation of their life and commitment to God and the community."

The *Senior Disciple* has served with distinction and is no longer actively making disciples as their primary focus. Based on their anointing, knowledge, and experience in disciple making, the *Senior Disciple* is an advisor and counselor to the disciple-making community, especially the *Adult Disciples*. The *Senior Disciple* is a teacher, primarily of advanced-level teachings. The *Senior Disciples* must be respected because it was earned through the example they set for the community and sought after by the community. This is the only stage where physical age can be a factor. It cannot be that every elderly person is a *Senior Disciple* because physical age can impact the ability of a disciple to serve in some capacities. Transition from active ministry allows the *Senior Disciple* to become a counselor and teacher to the community to aid in nurturing other disciples. The *Senior Disciple* learns by allowing the community to care for them and honor them continually for their service. The community must rely on the *Senior Disciples* because the *Adult Disciples* do not know everything.

MINISTRY LEVEL

The *Senior Disciples* are teachers, mentors, and counselors to the *Adult Disciples*. They will also teach the community but will always correct and mentor the *Adult Disciples* – the pastors, bishops, apostles and elders. They do not have to serve in these roles, but there should be some who do.

Outline

In this stage you will demonstrate the following 6 characteristics by journaling your failures.

Every time you fail to demonstrate a characteristic, you will journal the experience and share it with the group. James 1:22-25 instructs disciples to be doers, not just hearers, of the word. Read this scripture at the beginning of each group meeting during this stage.

> "But be doers of the word and not merely hearers who deceive themselves. For if any are hearers of the word and not doers, they are like those who look at themselves in a mirror; for they look at themselves and, on going away, immediately forget what they were like. But those who look into the perfect law, the law of liberty, and persevere, being not hearers who forget but doers who act—they will be blessed in their doing." James 1: 22-25 NRSV

You are to demonstrate all six of these characteristics for the next six weeks:

- **Accountability** – You must embrace the power and freedom of confession. Tell on yourself. Secrets are not good. Disciples are liberated and governed by the truth; therefore, be accountable by telling the truth about yourself. When you have done wrong or failed to represent Yeshua – tell it. Get an accountability partner from within the group. Share your struggles, successes, and failures with your partner. You will only share failures with the group. In the group meeting, the group leader is the only one who can respond to failures; everyone else can only listen.

Remember the power and application of grace. As mature Disciples, you must demonstrate the ability to give grace before judgment.

- **Prayer** – You should have been developing your personal prayer life since the first stage. Now you will pray with and for others. Each week, pray with and for five people. You can only pray with and for the same person twice during this stage.
- **Punctuality** – It is time to start demonstrating responsibility. After this stage,

you will prepare to lead others, but this begins with being willing to lead yourself. Punctuality is demonstrated in two ways:

- Arriving on time or at least fifteen minutes early,
- Completing assignments and tasks excellently and ahead of time. This must be especially true for the things you do for God and the spiritual community..

- **Help** – Offer yourself to assist someone. This does not have to be planned. Learn to observe your surroundings and be mindful of whom God wants you to help. Help can be expressed in several different ways. Challenge yourself to get creative in the help you give.

- **Giving** – You will strive to become a giver *led* by the Holy Spirit. Some Disciples do not apply the effort to form discipline in our habits. Make the necessary changes to make the tenth your minimum, then seek the Holy

Spirit for the amount you are to give above the tenth.

- **Evangelism** – As a Disciple *Evangelism* is a lifestyle, not a ministry. You are to carry the gospel message everywhere by always being willing to cultivate New Disciples.

At this final stage of this journey, you cannot just go through the motions. Your group leader can take the group back to any stage you may be struggling to implement. Group leaders are responsible to God for the Disciples they cultivate. If they just let you proceed without demonstrating growth, they are accountable to God. As a group, challenge each other to demonstrate growth and stay together until each of you is ready to be a *Disciple Maker*.

NOTES

What is needed to be a Community Making Disciple?

- Evangelists **are interacting with Unborn Again people who need to:**
- Acknowledge Yeshua as their Savior and Lord.
- Commit to become a Disciple who is being prepared to be a *Disciple Maker*.
- A person who has already acknowledged Yeshua can start at the commitment to Disciple Making.
- **Teachers are those who focus on grace, prayer, and scripture reading for New Disciples.** These teachers will not mention or apply exegesis. The new Disciple must learn to be consistent in prayer and scripture reading. These teachers will lead the New Disciples Study and live alongside the new Disciple to help them address life issues. The Bible Reading plan on the mobile app should

be used for scripture reading. A record is to be kept with the starting date so we will know the completion date. These teachers are to progress the New Disciples through this development stage.

In order to be a teacher of New Disciples, they must demonstrate a firm knowledge of grace, forgiveness, prayer, and consistency in scripture reading.

- **Mentors for the Early Development stage.** The new Disciple is promoted to the Early Development stage where they are assigned a mentor. These mentors will have the most direct interaction with the new Disciple. The mentor must have a plan that exposes the new Disciple to living as a Disciple. The new Disciple must observe the life of their mentor. They interact spiritually and personally. These mentors need to be trained and have a consistent plan for interaction with their assigned Disciples. Mentors are to be supervised and required to give regular updates on their progress. There should be a monthly meeting where the mentors report and are evaluated to ensure they are managing their relationships successfully.

- **When the young Disciple is ready** to be promoted to the *Middle Disciple Stage*, **they will start to assist their mentor** with Disciples who are promoted to the Early Disciple Stage. This will give them limited responsibility while allowing the mentors to work with more Disciples in the Early Development Stage.

- **For the Adolescent Disciples, there must be a care team for the sick and elderly**. This care team should be part of

    outreach. They must visit and address the needs of the sick and elderly in the community but can also do this for people outside of the community. The *Adolescent Disciple* will be able to contact their mentor when needed, but they have been promoted from needing regular interaction with a mentor. They are now implementing what they have learned by caring for the sick and elderly. They will have a supervisor to assign tasks and evaluate progress.

- **Facilitators for Disciple Development Lifecycle Groups**

    As Disciples mature in this lifecycle, they should be transitioned to facilitate a group. This transition is best while they are still in a group. This will make allowances for their group facilitator to be their mentor. This is a lifecycle because it is intended to perpetuate itself. Spiritual development must be presented as a lifelong pursuit. Disciples are committed to self-development and development of the Disciples in the spiritual community. No one in the community is complacent or stagnant. Everyone is being challenged to grow through relationships and spiritual guidance. The DDL group facilitators should be produced from this lifecycle.

- **There Must be Evangelism Training and Opportunities for the Early Adult Development Stage**. The *Early Adult Disciples* must demonstrate an eagerness to reach the lost. While they are still growing, they must start making more Disciples through *Evangelism*. The *Evangelism* training and experiences must be structured and informed. The leaders in *Evangelism* must understand the methods of *Evangelism* that the community employs and be able to demonstrate them to the *Early Adult Disciples*. The teachers of *Evangelism* must remember that the *Early Adult Disciples* are being trained for *Evangelism*. They must be taught and allowed to serve alongside an experienced evangelist.

- **Seniors who have agreed to mentor the Adult Disciples with their experience**. The *Adult Disciple* must use the *Senior Disciples* to share struggles and the weight of their responsibility in the community. These *Senior Disciples* must maintain confidentiality and understand that Disciples are not perfect. They must mentor the *Adult Disciples* as they lead the community in various ways.

Acknowledgements

Thank you to my wonderful wife, Barbara J. Fite. Your support and partnership continues to encourage me to trust this vision more everyday.

Thank you to our children, Jerret and Andrea Fite; Torey and Jeanay Floyd; our wonderful grandchildren, Jeremiah, Hezekiah, Elijah, Aaron and Maya - you inspire me to press further and deeper to represent God to you and the world.

Thank you with great gratitude to my sister, Yvonne Nesbit. Your investment continues to bless my life and ministry.

My brothers and family - stay strong, together, and focused on the Kingdom of God.

Dr. Pazanta H. Byars, Ed.D - your investment is greatly appreciated. Your commitment to excellence is evident in this project.

Blessed Harvest Nation - we are on this great journey together to glorify Adonai through Yeshua. We are making *Disciples* of all nations. I am so thankful to journey with each of you.

To everyone who experiences this journey – remember this is a lifecycle because you must invest these teachings into others so that the journey never ends.